Proven
Methods
To BETTER

GRADES

Angelo F. Gadaleto, Ph.D.

Professor Emeritus

Academic Success Skills
High School and College
A College Readiness Program

Proven Methods to Better Grades ®

Book purchases and Licensing Agreements to use and share the online version of the program is available to schools. Inquires@provenmethods.net   Tel. (610)-717-4233

Postal Address:
Proven Methods to Better Grades, LLC
307 McIntosh Road
West Chester, PA 19382
USA

Online Version with Video Presentations available at
https://www.provenmethodstobettergrades.com

This Companion Book Is Designed For Use With or Without the Video Version of The Program

Academic Success Skills
High School and College
A College Readiness Program

Note To Students

Your academic success not only helps define your self-image and peer status but also is a critical factor affecting future opportunities with college and employment. The lessons of this program will teach you "State of the Art" techniques for efficient learning. You will learn to study smart, not necessarily harder, or longer. It is true that by using the right methods, you can learn more, learn better, and in less time. The value of the program was highlighted by a student who wrote in her evaluation of the program "why wasn't I taught these techniques sooner, it makes learning so much easier."

If you are already achieving A's and B's, the methods taught will provide you with strategies that make the process of earning excellent grades more comfortable. If you struggle with motivation or have mediocre study skills and, as a result, have not earned good grades, completion of this course can put you on the path to consistent success. The ease of using the methods and the academic success which comes from applying them will make the time you spend on academics more productive and rewarding.

This comprehensive program will teach you strategic approaches for learning new material, building long-term memory, and maximizing your test-taking skills. Many tools for learning like speed reading, alternative methods of taking notes, and getting the most out of time spent in class are all part of this program. The bonus lesson on self-motivation will help you avoid procrastination and maintain a higher level of academic motivation. Approaches for task and time management will help you stay on goal and have more guilt-free time for fun.

Enjoy this journey of learning new ways to earn good grades with less anxiety and more confidence. Learning and applying the methods of this program will improve the overall quality of your life as a student.

How Best To Use The Program

The time you commit to completing the lessons of this program will pay huge dividends in the form of academic comfort and success. The 12 Lessons are equivalent to a one-credit college academic orientation course and, therefore, will require a commitment on your part to budget the time to complete the program. A spaced learning plan where you budget time to view one or two lessons at a sitting is the best approach to gain the most from the program. There are just too many good ideas presented for you to try to absorb the whole program in only a few sessions.

Academic Success Skills
High School and College

A College Readiness Program

Proven Methods To Better Grades

Program Contents   12 Easy Lessons

APPENDIX
FORMS WHICH MAY BE COPIED

Time Management Worksheet
Master Task Schedule Worksheet
Daily Priority Schedule Worksheet

Lesson: Organization
Task Management Skills

Organizational skills are essential to academic success. This lesson will focus on methods that will help you with self-management for the completion of tasks. The organizational strategies presented will enable you to plan and prioritize actions that put you on a path to earning better grades with more confidence and less stress.

Homework Versus Study Time

In High School, teachers often require homework, an assignment that is typically due at the next class meeting. An error many high school students make is they spend little or no time on academic preparation beyond assigned homework.

In College, unlike high school, the learning process will not be micromanaged with day-to-day homework assignments. Unfortunately, many new college students do not spend time on academic work because of the faulty assumption that if the instructor did not give specific homework for the next class, it is not necessary to spend time on academics.

Rather than deciding to spend time on academic work based on the question:
"Do I have homework.?"
A better approach is to answer the question:
"How do I best spend the time I have reserved for academics?"

How Do I Best Spend The Time Reserved For Academics

Method: Reserve Study Time For Review and Preparation Not Just Homework

The time you reserve for study should include homework assignments as well as the tasks of review and preparation.

Review: Repetition in the form of review is key to being ready for exams and for building long-term memory. The review process includes activities like reading over and clarifying the class notes you created. The longer you wait to review class notes, the less useful they become. Take a small block of time each day to strengthen the memory cues you acquired from having completed earlier reading assignments. The review of reading can be as simple as scanning your textbook table of contents and reading over the bold headings in your text.

Previewing: A strategically timed preview effort will reduce the overall time needed for learning and exam preparation. Previewing provides order, linkage of ideas, and establishes a foundation of memory cues that will help you retrieve content when you need it. A preview process will help you get the most from your classes. If you are taking a math or science class, for example, reading a few pages ahead will allow the teacher's presentation to clarify and reinforce content.

Reading: To be a successful student who consistently earns good grades, you must develop the practice of reading your textbooks. Trying to rely on only teacher lectures to master subject content is not a realistic practice. Most multiple-choice test questions used by your teachers come from test banks provided by textbook publishers. Part of your daily routine of study should include time to keep pace with the reading that corresponds to what is being taught in class.

**Use Study Time to (1) Complete Homework, (2) Review, And
(3) Prepare (Preview and Read)**

Method: Use Spaced Learning Techniques

Spaced learning is a process that divides the tasks of learning into manageable segments. You can view it as a divide and conquer approach. The method provides the opportunity for using memory building techniques that include Repetition and Reinforcement over time. Multiple exposures to the content you are trying to learn are necessary for building long term memory. The alternative, cramming, makes the challenge of learning and earning good grades much riskier. You may learn enough to get an acceptable grade on exams, but the rate of forgetting using the cramming method denies you the opportunity for true learning.

The use of task schedules, which set daily and weekly learning goals for each subject, gives you a competitive edge over students who rely on last-minute cramming techniques to prepare for exams.

Avoid Cramming

COMPARISON
CRAMMING VS SPACED LEARNING

Academic Task

What: Prepare for a mid-term exam covering 60 pages
When: Exam in 14 days

COMPARE

Student X who uses
Cramming Techniques

A student who uses the cramming technique might try to read and learn
60 pages in 2-3 days or less.
The student must average 20 or more pages a day with little time for repetition or review. Regardless of the grade achieved, forgetting will occur at a higher rate than with the Spaced Learning Approach.

IN CONTRAST TO

Student Y who uses
Task Management Technique of Spaced Learning

A student who uses Spaced Learning might divide the task into
Ten learning days and Four review days.
On Learning Days, the student sets a daily goal of completing an average of six pages of reading each day. Time each day is also used to review prior reading, which reinforces memory cues.

On Review Days, the student has time to go back over material that they have already read and reviewed previously. Learning over time with a systematic review process results in less forgetting with the ability to recall content long term.

Method: Maintain a Master-Task Schedule

A Master Task Schedule allows you to organize your academic tasks from a longer-term perspective and set realistic daily goals for study and review so you can complete all learning tasks and have adequate time for review before exams.

SAMPLE: MASTER TASK SCHEDULE

Subject	When Next Test Project Due	What Content To Be Tested	Reserved Review Days	Daily Task Goals
Math	14 Days	Chapters 4 & 5 25 Pages	2 Days	Review Homework Plus Read Avg. 2-3 pages
Science	21 Days	Chapters 7 40 Pages	4 Days	Review Homework Plus Read Avg. 2-3 pages
Foreign Language	7 Days	Unit 4 10 Pages	3 Days	Review Practice Plus Read Avg. 2-3 pages
History	14 Days	Chapters 13 & 14 60 Pages	4 Days	Review Work on Paper Project Plus Read Avg. 6 pages
English	18 Days	Chapters 9 & 10 90 Pages	3 Days	Review Homework Work on Paper Project Plus Read Avg. 6 pages

Steps For Creating Your Master Task Schedule

Step 1 Since your Master Task Schedule is a "To Do" system, list each subject.
Most students find it helpful to start their study time with the courses they find most challenging and save the easier courses for later in the study time allotted when energy might be lower.

Step 2 Note when the next test or project is due, how many days are available to get ready.
This information may be announced in class or found in the syllabus. If it is not clear when the exam will take place, you should ask the course instructor.

Step 3 Find out and list content that will be on the exam.
What chapters and how many pages will be included on the exam.

Step 4 Set aside a specific number of days to complete a systematic review.
Review days are different than learning days. During review days, you are going back over material you have already read and reviewed previously. Your goal is to refresh and reinforce memory cues established earlier.

Step 5 Determine a daily goal for each subject.
This daily goal includes activities such as reading, review, and study, in addition to any homework assigned. Having an established daily goal for reading allows for the flexibility to read less on some days and more on other days as you keep pace with completing all reading. To keep pace with the completion of papers and projects, you will want to identify and build tasks into your daily goals that will allow you to use the Spaced Learning Approach for completing these assignments.

Create A Master Task Schedule

Method: Use A Daily Priority Schedule

When making use of a daily priority schedule, you review your goals from your Master Task Schedule and make adjustments based on your immediate needs. If, for example, you found out you were going to have a quiz the following day in science, you might postpone your daily goal in English and double your time spent in science. Often a review of your study needs for the day will lead to an increase in the time you commit to your academics.

Sample
Daily Priority Schedule

Subject	Daily Goals From Master Task Schedule	Adjusted Goals Based on Priority Needs	Estimated Time To Complete	Notes
Math	Review Homework Plus Read Avg.2-3 pages	Review Homework Plus Read 3 pages	30 Minutes	
Science	Review Homework Plus Read Avg. 2-3 pages	Quiz Tomorrow Review & Study Chapter 7	60 Minutes	
Foreign Language	Review Practice Plus Read Avg.2-3 pages	Practice Conversation for Class Presentation Tomorrow Read 2 pages	20 Minutes	
History	Review Homework Work on Paper Project Plus Read Avg. 6 pages	Review Explore and Select Paper Topic Read 6 Pages	30 Minutes	
English	Review Homework Work on Paper Project Plus Read Avg. 6 pages	Review Find Resources for Paper Project Delay Reading	20 Minutes	
Other				

Discussion Questions:

How do you currently keep track of the academic work you need to complete?

What approach do you use to combat procrastination with your academics?

How would you describe your organizational skills with the academic work you need to complete?

Do you rely primarily on just a few days before an exam to prepare for the exam? If so, why?

What steps do you take to complete term papers and projects?

Which do you think will better help you learn and earn better grades, cramming, or using a Spaced Learning Approach, why?

NOTES

Lesson: Memory Skills
Part I

One of the reasons you may cram for exams rather than use spaced learning methods could be a lack of confidence in your long-term memory. Why study in advance if you believe you are just going to forget material soon after learning? Understanding how your memory works should guide your approach to study. Each section of this Proven Methods to Better Grades program describes memory building strategies that will help you effectively acquire new information and transfer what you learn from Short-Term to Long-Term memory.

If you just finished eating dinner and were asked to describe the meal, you could do so in great detail. However, if you were asked to describe what you had for dinner five days ago, you might have very little memory of the meal. Your ability to recall what you just ate is an example of Short-Term Memory. Whatever you remember from the meal you ate five days ago is an example of Long-Term memory. It is not essential to remember what you ate days ago, but when it comes to academic study, having material stored in long-term memory is the key to success.

There are two memory strategies to move information from your Short-Term to Long-Term Memory. One approach is Rote Memorization, which requires repetition and relies little on understanding or associations. Learning using the strategy of Understanding and Building Associations is easier than the rote memory approach and is a more efficient way to use your study time. When possible, it is better to use understanding and association approaches to build long-term memory. Both methods of building memory will be useful to you as a student. Some information just has to be learned by rote memorization. Effective Methods for using Rote Memorization to build memory are presented in the lesson: Memory Skills Part II.

This lesson will introduce you to a three-step memory development method that uses association strategy. The "SIR" (Survey-Input-Reinforce) Method described in this lesson is simple to implement but will give you powerful results. The approach provides you with a structure for learning that makes use of not only the learning principle of association but also uses the learning components of order, focus, repetition, and recall.

Whether you are using the Rote Memorization Methods or the more efficient Understanding and Association Methods, multiple exposures, and opportunities to test your recall of material are essential. The Spaced Learning Techniques described in The Task Management Lesson gives you the opportunity for multiple repetitions with time intervals between repetitions. A mantra the author often uses in this program is "Repetition and Recall" are the keys to learning.

The author of this program has used the understanding of how our memory works to create a Memory Step Approach to learning. The acronym "SIR" will help you learn and make use of recommended memory development steps. The SIR Memory Step Approach gives you order and structure in the learning process, which enables you to develop better linkages that will help you remember.

A Memory Step Approach

Step 1 **Survey** Tell Yourself In Advance What You Want To Learn
Create Memory Cues---Memory Anchors

Step 2 **Input** Be An Active Learner
Learn With Concentration

Step 3 **Reinforce** Ask Yourself What You Just Learned
Practice Recall Using Memory Cues
Multiple Repetitions

ACRONYM SIR

Step 1 Survey

The "S" represents Survey

When you survey what you want to learn, you gain a clear focus that helps build memory. The Survey process helps you create memory cues that are essential to the memory retrieval process.

Create Memory Cues (Retrieval Cues)

Stimulus Words, Keywords, or Questions, act as memory cues, also known as memory anchors that help you pull out memory when it is needed. When you have multiple memory cues, you get the benefit of linkage among cues, which is like using a net rather than a single rope to pull out a memory.

Apply The Survey Step With Textbooks
To Build Memory Cues-Memory Anchors

Most textbooks have a structure that will help you identify the focus of your learning. Start by taking the time to read the **Table Of Contents,** focusing on what the main topics are and how they are sequenced and linked. Before you read in your textbook, take the time to preview the **Titles and Subtitles,** which are usually in Bold Print. You can develop effective memory **linkages** if you reflect on the possible meaning of the **Titles and Subtitles** and create questions to be answered as you read. If your textbook provides a list of **learning objectives,** use them as a survey tool before reading. Reading the summary of a chapter before you read the chapter is also a powerful survey technique. The Reading Lesson in this program will go into more detail on how to use the survey process before reading.

Apply The Survey Step With Academic Classes
To Increase Understanding and Build Memory

Before attending class, seek ways to preview content that might be presented. If your teacher is following the content of a textbook, such as in a math class, read ahead so that you have a basic understanding before the teacher presents the material. If the teacher's lecture becomes a second exposure to the content, it will help you get more understanding and clarity from the class. You will find that concepts that were difficult to understand in class become easier to understand.

The process of previewing before class is an excellent example of how it is possible to learn more in less time. If you have previewed for class, the teacher's presentation becomes a powerful memory building reinforcement step, which reduces the number of additional repetitions needed.

Step 2   Input

The "I" represents Input
CONCENTRATION AND FOCUS
MAKING A CONSCIOUS EFFORT TO BUILD MEMORY

This "Input" step highlights methods for entering information into your memory. This second step is the core or center point of the learning process. You must be an active learner. If you are not making a conscious effort to remember the material, it is likely relearning will be necessary. You will want to continually strive for understanding and meaning to assimilate new facts into your long-term memory.

Step 3   <u>R</u>einforce

The "R" represents Reinforcement

RECALL AND REPETITION ARE KEYS TO LEARNING

RECALL is the process of testing your memory using memory cues or questions
REPETITION is the act of repeating, having multiple exposures

Your memory of new material will become more powerful if you make use of reinforcement techniques. Immediate and frequent recall, the process of answering the question, "what did I just learn?" is essential for developing strong memory. You will want to identify memory cues (stimulus words, stimulus phrases, keywords, or questions) that will make the process of future study with recall more efficient.

Repetitions will strengthen memory and make retrieving information an easy process. Repetitions, with time intervals between repetitions, make building long-term memory easier than trying to develop memory in one block of time.

Recall And Repetition With Time Intervals Between Repetitions
Is A Powerful Memory Building Method

Memory and Lifestyle Choices

Sleep and Memory

Improving your memory is often a matter of lifestyle. Getting adequate rest and sleep is a major factor that helps memory formation. Studying when you are tired or sleepy is self-defeating. Getting adequate sleep can be a challenge, but you should consider it an important priority. There are individual differences in requirements for sleep, but most students require 8 hours give or take an hour. When you get behind on your sleep requirements, a sleep deficit exists, which will have a detrimental effect on your memory.

A luxury you may have in College, where on average, you only attend classes 3-4 hours a day, is the opportunity to take a short nap. Keep any naps to under an hour; longer naps can be detrimental. Even a short power nap of 20 minutes will help your memory power. A nap can help you more than trying to treat your fatigue with caffeine drinks.

Diet and Exercise

A proper diet can have a positive impact on brain function and memory. Unhealthy diets that include a lot of junk food can adversely affect your cognitive skills. Drinks that are high in sugar like soda interfere with your brain getting the even flow of glucose it needs to work at its best. Any food that spikes your blood sugar will cause a dip in your brain's function later. Make it a habit of drinking water throughout the day to keep fully hydrated, which helps memory. Foods like fruits, vegetables, eggs, and food rich in omega-3 fatty acids are good for your brain function. Keeping your blood-sugar levels steady throughout the day will help your academic performance. It is not a good habit to skip breakfast. Eating frequent smaller meals and avoiding large meals, especially late at night, is better for memory function.

There is a lot of evidence that indicates aerobic exercise can improve your memory function. Exercise boosts blood flow to areas of the brain involved in memory. Regular exercise will increase your energy and help you avoid fatigue. Make physical activity an important part of your lifestyle.

Alcohol and other drug use and their relationship to academic achievement

It hopefully does not surprise you to be told that there is clear evidence that shows students with higher grades are less likely to use and abuse alcohol or other drugs. Alcohol and academics are a bad mix. If you choose to drink, it is important to your potential of success that you make intelligent decisions as to when and how much you drink to minimize the negative effects on your academics. Excessive drinking, getting drunk, can have lingering effects on your memory. Be aware that even small amounts of alcohol can hinder the ability of the brain to transfer information from your short-term to long-term memory.

Discussion Questions:

What Actions do you take when you want to remember something?

When you meet someone new, what process do you use to remember their name?

What do you see as the parallels between practice in sports and preparation for exams?

Why do some of your memories last longer than other memories?

Why do you forget some things and not others?

Do you believe the emotions surrounding an event will impact your ability to remember?

Give an example of when a clue helped you remember information?

What are the most effective ways you can remember information for exams?

NOTES

Lesson: Concentration

Enhance Your Ability to Maintain Focus

Your ability to develop memory requires concentration. Paying attention to what you are trying to learn, giving it your undivided attention, is not automatic, and requires a conscious effort and commitment on your part. There are many factors related to your environment, and your physical condition that can interfere with your ability to concentrate. Different learning situations require alternative concentration approaches. The length of time you can maintain a sharp focus will fluctuate depending on factors that this lesson will help you understand.

Motivating yourself to develop the commitment and habit of intense concentration is easier when you recognize the reward of earning better grades in less time. A sharp focus will reduce the number of repetitions required for you to move what you learn from your short-term to long-term memory. Less time is needed to review before an exam because you do not have to relearn the material.

A method developed by the author of this program for maximizing your concentration uses a system of "Concentration Blocks" that allow for the uniqueness of the learning situation. The method will provide you with an approach for recycling your concentration and help you maximize the rewards of the time you spend studying.

Method: Make Use of Concentration Blocks

The use of concentration blocks is a strategic approach that will maximize the return you get from the time and effort you put in to study. The success of study time should be measured not in how long you study but rather on how much you learn when you do study. Your ability to maintain a high level of concentration over time is limited. It is not unusual for students to sit down to study and find that after a short period, their concentration wanes, and they find themselves dividing their attention with something else. Concentration Blocks keep you focused and utilize the highly effective three-step memory building process "SIR" -**S**urvey-**I**nput-**R**einforce.

Concentration Blocks

The Concentration Block approach has you divide more extended units of Time or Task into smaller "Concentration segments." You would then refresh your focus with each time unit or task segment. The goal is to build a better memory of the content by maintaining a high level of concentration. The length of your concentration blocks should correspond to your ability to maintain focus. You want to avoid spending time when your attention level is not productive in building memory.

In the example below, let's assume you have committed an hour to study content that is moderately challenging to understand. You make the judgment that it would be productive to recycle your concentration about every twenty minutes. Before beginning each concentration block, you would survey (preview) what you are about to study and renew your motivation to concentrate. For the next twenty minutes, you give the content your undivided attention. At the end of each concentration block, you would test your recall to the content of what you just studied. This recall process helps build long-term memory and allows you to monitor the actual level of your concentration.

Concentration Block Example Using Time

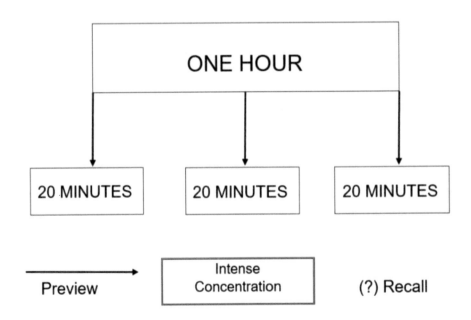

You Recycle Your Concentration With Each Block
Use Memory Steps with Each Block

Method: Mentally Prepare to Concentrate

Develop a Positive Attitude. Get rid of negative thoughts that interfere with your ability to concentrate. You can reshape negative attitudes into positive attitudes. Your negative feelings toward a subject or teacher come from your thoughts. A major theory in psychology uses the premise that by controlling your thoughts, you control your feelings.

You can change your thinking →You control your thoughts
Example: Instead of thinking "I hate math, I can't do math."
  Think/tell yourself, "Math is not so bad, I can do it if I try hard."

Develop An Interest. It is easier to concentrate when you have an interest in what you are learning. It is beneficial, therefore, to foster an interest in the subjects you are trying to learn. Some possible ways to increase interest:

- Learn about the authors and their motivation for writing about the topic.
- Attempt to relate what you are learning to your everyday life.
- Imagine how you would use the information you are learning in your future work life.

Method: Study in a Location Conducive to Learning

Study in a Quiet Place that has Minimal Distractions. You need quiet to study. You should avoid distractions like television, radio, social media, and people talking. You cannot effectively learn if you are trying to focus on two or more things at the same time.

Caution: For most students, any background music (although it may be comfortable or enjoyable) is harmful to the memory process. If you attempt to use background music to filter out other sounds, it must be soft music. If you are listening to the words of a song, you are not giving your undivided attention to what you are studying.

Don't be too Comfortable. Have you ever fallen asleep while studying? You were most likely studying in a comfortable chair, couch, or even your bed. The place of study that is usually most productive may not be the most comfortable. There is a reason the classical workspace is a desk/chair or table/chair arrangement.

Study In a Well Ventilated Place. It is difficult to concentrate in a hot or stuffy room. It is better when your place of study is cool rather than warm to facilitate concentration.

Use Proper Lighting. Bright light can cause glare; dull light can cause eye strain, which interferes with the learning process. A proper study lamp uses low WATT white light and is comfortable to the eyes. Most Library study areas and College Residence Hall study areas have proper lighting.

Caution: It may not be possible for you to study effectively in the place you find most convenient. Be honest with yourself, if your current place of study is not conducive to concentration, find a better place. Libraries and designated study areas can help you achieve the goal of quality study time.

Discussion Questions

What helps you concentrate when you are studying?

What factors interfere with your ability to concentrate when studying?

What are the places you use to study that helps you concentrate best?

Does listening to music while studying help or hinder your ability to concentrate?

How can you increase your interest in what you are studying?

How can you control your attitude toward studying a subject?

NOTES

Lesson: Time Management

A Tool For Balance, Well-Being, and Success

Most of the Proven Methods to Better Grades program is about the "Quality of Study." This critically important lesson is about the "Quantity of Time" needed to reach your goals. A big challenge for you as a student will be to find enough time to do all that you should do and would like to do. Time is a limited resource, and your job is to spend it wisely. If you want to be academically successful and also want to maximize your enjoyment in your life, you must learn the skill of budgeting your time. The schedule you develop should reflect your commitment to the job of being a highly successful student. An effective time management schedule is a tool for more than scheduling work; it also makes time for enjoyable, satisfying, and rejuvenating activities. A properly developed time management plan will give you the balance of adequate time for academic preparation and the joy of guilt-free fun time. The time management skills you learn in school will serve you all of your life.

Why budget your time? The simple answer is that if you do not, you will most likely fail to reach your academic goals. Prior Proper Planning is what prevents disappointing results. There will be many activities competing for your time. It is human nature for you to spend your time doing that, which is most enjoyable unless you have accepted and value the fact that there is a compelling reason to do otherwise. Your time management schedule will provide you with a Work-Play Balance and keep you on the path to success.

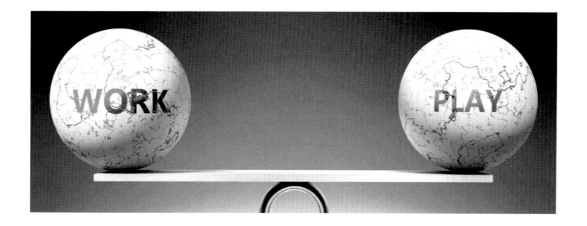

Your Time Management Plan Should Provide A Balance Between Academic Work and Time for Guilt-Free Fun

Method: Set A Goal For A Minimum Of Study Time Each Week

Guidelines for the
Amount of Study Time Needed

The author of this program, based on his years of experience working to help students be successful, has developed guidelines for Minimum Amounts of scheduled study time for both High School and College students. Study Time in the author's guidelines includes all time spent on academic work outside of class time, including homework, review, preparation, reading, as well as time spent on projects and papers. Making and maintaining the commitment to A Minimum Amount Of Study Time Each Week will help you avoid the habit of relying on cramming as an approach to academic preparation.

A commitment to a minimum number of study hours will help you establish a pattern of when you study. If you make the specific times you set aside for academics a habit, you will be able to deal more effectively with activities that compete for your time. If, for example, part of your reserved study time is 7 to 9 PM each evening, Sunday through Thursday, it will be much easier to avoid competing activities like watching television or socializing with your friends during this time. You can always add more time to your established study blocks, but you should strive to reach your minimum goals for study time each week. If you miss a study block, make it a goal to make up the lost study time.

If you did an online search for study time recommendations, you would get a wide range of answers. Most suggestions for College students are to spend two or three hours on academic preparation time for each academic credit. This recommendation would require you to spend six to nine hours for each three-credit course. Many College students who earn high grades do study these many hours. However, these are ambitious study time goals that are difficult for many students to achieve. The amount of study time you will need for each course will differ depending on the rigors of the course and the requirements of your instructor. It is better to establish A Realistic Minimum Amount of Study Time Each Week that you believe is proper and realistic for you.

Establish A Pattern of Study   Make Your Study Times A Habit

Guidelines for High School Study Time

High School Is A Great Time To Build And Practice Time Management Skills, So You Are Better Prepared For The Transition To College.

The typical High School student who has a desire to earn A/B grades should schedule a MINIMUM EVERY WEEK of 8 to 10 hours of study time outside of school. Many factors determine how much study time you need each week. If your goal is to earn higher grades, you will want to study more than the minimum required. You must have time to review and prepare for your classes in addition to just having time to complete homework assignments. Honors and AP classes will require more time than less demanding courses. When you aim high, you must find the time to support your goal of excellence. You will get better results when you use proven study methods, but you still need to devote adequate time to reach your goals.

Guidelines for College Study Time

The typical College student who has a desire to earn A/B grades should, in the opinion of the author, schedule a MINIMUM -EVERY WEEK of 20 hours of study time outside of class. High school students making the transition to College need to understand that the expectation in higher education is that students spend significant time reading and studying outside of class.

A comparison of structured class times in High School and College will help you understand the need for significantly more reserved time for study at College.

Comparison of High School and College Weekly Schedules

Structured Time

High School	College
35 Hours a Week	**15-18 Hours a Week**
[Five Days -Seven hours a Day]	[Five/Six Courses each with three hours of class]

Full-time college students have approximately <u>20 Fewer Hours</u> of structured in school time. If you want to be successful in College, you must use this difference in structured time for study activities. The process of learning in College involves much more independent learning.

Time Devoted To Study and
Your Likelihood Of Academic Success

So what should your weekly goal for study time be as a college student? Only you can answer this question based on your dedication, the work demands of your courses, and how much time you can make available for study. The earlier you get started and the better planned your Task Management approach, which uses Spaced Learning, the easier the task. To help you with your study decisions, the author of this program is providing this Chart that shares the "Likelihood of Academic Success" based on his research and work experience with college students.

Guidelines for Weekly College Study
Assumes You Start From Week One And Do Not Skip Weeks

Full-Time College Student 15 to 18 Academic Credits
Five or Six Academic Courses

Minimum Weekly Goals (Every Week!)		Likelihood of Academic Success
Less Than 12 Hours	Time budgeted for study weekly	Low
12 to 15 Hours	Time budgeted for study weekly	Possible/Risky
15 to 19 Hours	Time budgeted for study weekly	Better
20-24 Hours	Time budgeted for study weekly	Good/Very Good
25 Hours or More	Time budgeted for study weekly	Excellent

Part-Time College Student

Minimum Weekly Goals (Every Week!) For Each Three Credit Course		Likelihood of Academic Success
Less Than 2.5 Hours	Time budgeted for study weekly	Low
2.5 to 3 Hours	Time budgeted for study weekly	Possible/Risky
3 to 4 Hours	Time budgeted for study weekly	Better
4 to 5 Hours	Time budgeted for study weekly	Good/Very Good
5 Hours or More	Time budgeted for study weekly	Excellent

Method: Make Use of 6 or 7 days to reach your goal For Study Time each Week

The more days you use to complete your study goals, the less pressure you will feel. You are more likely to reach your weekly study goals if the daily average of planned study is reasonable.

High School Example

Goal: A Minimum of Ten Hours of Study For The Week

If you have planned study sessions <u>four days a week</u>
Two and Half hours are required each day to reach your goal

If you planned study sessions <u>seven days a week</u>
Less than 90 Minutes a day would be required to reach your goals

College Example

Goal: A Minimum of 20 Hours of Study For The Week

If you have planned study sessions <u>four days a week</u>
Five hours are required each day to reach your goal

If you planned study sessions <u>seven days a week</u>
Less than three hours a day would be required to reach your goals

A four-day academic schedule makes it difficult for you to apply the time management methods recommended in this program. If, however, you made time Friday, Saturday, and Sunday to study your entire week becomes less stressful and more enjoyable.

Use of 6 or 7 days to reach Your Weekly Study Goals

Consider the following example scenario that shows a College student making use of a seven-day schedule to Accomplish 22 Hours of Study In A Week

Monday-Thursday: The student schedules one or two study sessions a day- An average of three hours a day. Besides, regularly scheduled daily study blocks, an additional 2-3 hours of preparation a week, could be accomplished using the time before, between, or after classes.

Friday: Before the student starts the weekend, they spent 2 hours studying using the time before, between, or after classes or a study block in the early or late afternoon.

Saturday: After sleeping late, the student spends two hours studying, perhaps late morning into the early afternoon. Saturday late afternoon and the evening are free to socialize or spend time at a part-time job.

Sunday: The student spends the day relaxing but is sure to make a 7 PM – 10 PM study block a priority.

Method: Identify time robbers

Keep Track and Analyze how you spend your time.

Before you attempt to change how you spend your time, you need an accurate understanding of how you use your time.

As a step in developing your time management schedule, you are encouraged to examine what is consuming your time and decide if the activity is consistent with your priority of earning excellent grades. Often activities like watching television, social media, gaming, or socializing with friends monopolize much of a student's time. Finding enough time for study may require that you make changes. Making sufficient study time a high priority is a key to your academic success.

What Are Your Time Robbers

Method: Determine Priorities
Make decisions about the most beneficial use of your time.

Working and going to school is necessary for many students. How much you work must take into account the necessity to study for academic success. Depending on your ability to find time for study, you may have to reduce the time you spend working. An alternative as a college student is the option to take fewer courses in a semester. You must face the fact that learning and earning good grades will require adequate reserved time for study.

Although it is positive to belong to clubs, organizations, and sports teams, it is self-defeating to engage in so many activities that you do not have time to study.

Every student has "Must Do" activities like eating and sleeping. Commuter students, students who work, older, non-traditional students, students with parental responsibility, all have unique obligations. The time demands of full-time students will differ based on issues like work, involvement in sports, and other life choice activities. The more demands you have on your time, the more critical it is that you make and reserve adequate time for study.

Method: Develop A Pattern Of Study

Make your study times a habit. Attempt to study the same times each day of the week. When you study at the same time regularly, you will be better able to combat activities that compete for your time. If on school days you commit to studying from seven to nine in the evening, television shows in that time block will become easier to avoid.

As a **High School Student**, the seven-hour school day will limit your choices of time blocks for study. Your block of reserved study time can be after school in the late afternoon or after dinner in the early evening. You will want to avoid late-night study when fatigue can be a factor. Many successful high school students commit to an either-or situation "I will complete my study block before dinner or after depending on what the competition is for my time." It will become more comfortable to reach your weekly study goals if you have reserved time for study on the weekends. If, for example, you make a habit of having a study block Sunday evenings, you will be better ready to start your academic week and reach your weekly goals for study time.

College Students have the opportunity to develop a pattern of study mornings, afternoons, or evenings based on their class schedule. As noted earlier, instead of having seven hours of structured school time as in high school, the typical college class schedule will involve an average of three to four hours a day. Many high school students, when they make the transition to College, discover that a productive time for their study includes early hours. If, for example, your college class schedule Monday, Wednesday, and Friday has classes starting at 11 AM, an excellent time for a study block on those days could be 8:30 AM to 10:30 AM.

If you devote the period of 7 to 9:30 PM to one of your daily study blocks, you could have the opportunity of using afternoon and early evening hours for work, sports, or a guilt-free fun time. Your friends will come to understand that you are available before 7 PM or after 9:30 PM, but not during the time you have reserved for study.

Method: Avoid Long Blocks Of Study

If you try to study for long periods without adequate break time, you will get diminishing returns. If you have a study block that will last more than two hours, plan a short break to refresh your energy.

Method: (In College) Use Time Before, Between and After Classes

There are often significant gaps of time between classes in College. Making use of these time gaps will help you reach your weekly study goals. On most college campuses, it is easy to find a location to study that is close to your next class.

For lecture classes, it is advantageous to review the context of your notes right <u>after</u> class. For recitation classes, such as language classes, it is beneficial to preview right <u>before</u> class.

Method: Make Use of a Time Planner to Schedule and Monitor Your Time

The planner tool you use to organize and manage your time is the backbone of your organizational efforts. Investing time and effort with your planner will provide you with the guidance you need to make the most efficient and effective use of your time. A useful planner tool will enable you to plan and monitor your time daily, weekly, and long-term. When you work with a planner, you have a master list of how you have decided to spend your time best. You have a time map that will lead you to your goal of achieving the best grades possible.

Keep in mind that making use of a planner allows you to plan your time and also monitor your time. There will be situations when you have to make adjustments to the master plan you have developed. It is helpful to think of your planner as a guidance tool. Even when you have a strong motivation to adhere to your schedule, events might alter how you spend your time. There will be times when your desire to play will win out over your goals for work. Having your planner with time goals listed allows you to make modifications when needed. If, for whatever reason, you do not use a block of time you had reserved for study, the monitoring process, allows you to add a make-up study block at a later time.

Available in Appendix of This Book

Time Management Worksheet
Master Task Schedule Worksheet
Daily Priority Worksheet

(Worksheets May Be Copied)

Discussion Questions:

How would you describe your time management skills?

What process do you use to manage your time?

How much time do you believe you should reserve for academic activities outside of school?

Do you make time to complete academic work on weekends? If so, when do you do so?

When was the last time you used time early in the day for academic work?

Do you make it a habit to study the same times each day? If so, when do you do so?

NOTES

Lesson: Reading For Speed and Retention

Reading is a critical tool for successful learning. In this lesson, you will examine your reading habits. It will be easier to improve your reading skills if you understand your current reading practices. Your goal will be to improve your reading efficiency by increasing your overall reading speed and the amount you learn when you read. Reading requirements increase as you advance in school and as the responsibility for learning shifts from the instructor to the student. One of the notable differences between high school academics and college academics is the amount you must read if you are to maximize your success as a student.

Readings Is A Skill That Can Be Improved

Your goal should be to understand and retain content while reading at the fastest speed that allows that to happen.

Method: Understand and Apply Strategies for Increasing Your Reading Speed

Do you read for entertainment and pleasure? Do you enjoy reading the daily newspaper, magazine articles, or novels? If you can answer yes to these questions, you no doubt have a head start in learning how to be a faster reader. Recreational reading, by its very nature, fosters a higher rate of speed when reading.

Developing advanced reading skills often starts with changing practices you developed as a child. Most of us, as children, learned to read with methods that encouraged the reading of one word at a time. Reading out loud, as a process, involves focusing on one word at a time. If you have the habit of mouthing words as you read, you will want to change this practice.

You can think much faster than you can talk, so it is vital to break the habit of reading at a self-talk pace.

Speed reading programs start with the simple premise that you should focus on 2-3 or more words at a time. You need to learn that reading is a mental process, not a verbal process. When reading, it is possible to sight-read groups of words at a time and still absorb the meaning of the words. If you increase your average eye fixation from one word to three words, you will achieve a 300% increase in your reading speed.

Example: How focusing on more words with each eye fixation can increase reading speed

The/cost/of/wheat/has/risen/because/of/the/drought.

vs

The cost of wheat/has risen/because of/the drought.

(Better Yet)

The cost of wheat/ has risen/because of the drought.

The pace of your reading will increase when you develop the habit of mentally focusing on groups of words at a time.

Method: Practice Increasing Reading Speed

One of the best ways to learn to read faster is to force yourself
to pick-up the speed at which you read.

To increase your reading speed, devote 15 minutes a day to practicing speed drills. A recommended exercise is to read a paragraph at your current average pace and then test your understanding and recall to the content of the paragraph. Next, read another comparable paragraph and consciously force yourself to read it faster than your comfort level and again test your understanding and recall. Many students find that with practice, they understand and recall more, not less when they force themselves to read faster. If you practice a faster pace of reading, you can create a new, more rapid rate of speed when reading.

Highlighting Textbooks

A difference in College from High School is that you typically must purchase and, therefore, will own your textbooks. Highlighting in your text can be an effective way to create memory cues. You will not want the process of highlighting to slow down your reading rate. An effective procedure is to complete reading an entire paragraph or more before you go back and selectively highlight. Key things to highlight are words that provide a memory cue to main ideas. You might highlight terms, dates, names, definitions, or any words with which you are not familiar.

Do not use highlighting as a method to pace your reading. If you want a pacing instrument to help with reading, use a ruler or index card. As a guideline, you should highlight no more than 5 to 10 percent of what you are reading. Check the usefulness of your highlighting procedure by going back and testing your recall of what you read by looking only at what you highlighted.

Method: Apply Memory Steps With Academic Reading

The benefit of academic reading should be measured not in how long or how much you read but rather on how much you retain from what you have read. You want to avoid having to reread material multiple times to make it part of your long-term memory. Your goal is to learn more in less time by using the strategic memory step approach of Survey, Input, and Reinforcement (SIR) when reading.

You should avoid reading academic content, in the same manner, that you read recreational material. When you read for pleasure, there is no need to be concerned with concentration, or your ability to transfer what you are reading from your short-term to long-term memory. Academic reading to be most effective requires a high degree of concentration and should use a structured approach that enables you to develop better linkages and memory anchors.

How to Read Academic Material

Step One: Survey

"Tell Yourself In Advance What It Is You Want To Learn As You Read"

Most textbooks use a structure that helps students select the most important content to focus on and learn. If you survey in advance, what it is you are about to read, you can develop an order to the content and build memory cues that act as memory anchors. If you learn memory cues at the same time you learn new information, it will help you retrieve what you need to know from your memory. Making use of the survey opportunities listed below will help you understand and retain more of what you learn from reading.

Survey opportunities when reading a textbook

- Study the Table of Contents. Take a moment to reflect on your understanding and the meaning inferred in the titles and headings. How does the chapter you are about to read fit in with other chapters of the text or major sections of the text? How is the chapter information organized?

- Continue your preview of the chapter by reading any study aids that are part of the chapter, like listings of learning objectives, discussion questions, exercises, or activities.

- Look over the visual aids in the chapter, such as pictures, charts, and graphs.

- If the chapter has an introduction section or if it has a summary, read them before you read the chapter to understand better what the author considers most important.

- Read with an active focus by using chapter headings or subheadings to create questions that you try to answer as you read.

- If you have class notes on the subject, review these notes before you read to gain an understanding of what your teacher considers most important.

Step Two: Input "Be An Active Reader."

After completing the first step of organizing in your mind what it is you are trying to learn, it is time to start the Input process of active reading. The Survey Process has given you definite ideas and answers to look for as you read. In addition to questions you have formulated, make use of any printed learning objectives or questions the author has provided. Active reading requires concentration with an undivided clear focus on the content of what you are reading. Dividing a long block of reading into shorter concentration segments will give you more opportunities to establish memory cues and practice immediate recall.

Step Three: Reinforce, Ask Yourself, "What Did I just Read?"
Recall and Repetition are the Keys to Learning

Most forgetting occurs soon after initial exposure unless you use methods of Reinforcement. Immediate and frequent recall, the process of answering the question, "what did I just learn?" is essential for developing memory.

Multiple repetitions facilitate content learned to go from your short-term memory to long-term memory. The survey process creates memory cues that act as a stimulus that will help you retrieve information from your long-term memory. Creating and answering questions as you read based on headings and subheadings serves to both establish memory and give you the multiple exposures needed for developing a workable long-term memory. Repetition and Reinforcement take place whenever you read or reread the memory cues you have learned and test your ability to recall information using these cues.

Method: Vary Your Reading Speed

The purpose for which you are reading and the level of challenge you have in understanding the material should govern the rate at which you read. Reasons you may read faster or even skim the content might include getting a preliminary overview of a chapter, reviewing a section, trying to locate specific information, or just to get the general idea of the content. Most of your text reading will involve using your normal academic reading pace, which is the fastest pace that allows you to have a high level of comprehension. When reading complex information, you will want to slow down your reading to help with concentration and comprehension.

Vary Your Reading Speed

Skimming Technique

Skimming is a process where you selectively read portions of the content rapidly but strive to identify the main points or meaning the author is trying to convey. There are times when skimming, which allows you to cover a lot of material in less depth, is the right choice. You can read the table of contents, available summaries, headings, and subheadings as you skim, which will highlight major points. When skimming, it is a good idea to look over charts, diagrams, or pictures that may help point out the purpose of the author. Reading the first and last few paragraphs of a chapter before you skim the chapter will help you decide what is most important to read and what can be skipped. Read the first sentence of paragraphs, which usually serve as topic sentences. After this initial sentence, skip through the paragraph looking for what might be important pieces of information like places, names, or dates. After you have skimmed a section, pause and ask yourself to recall the main ideas you got out of the skimming process.

Rapid Reading

Do not get into the habit of reading all your academic material at the same pace. There will be many situations when rapid reading is the best choice. The conscious decision you make to accelerate or slow down the speed of your reading can be applied to the entire reading task or to just selected portions of the reading. The purpose and desired outcome of your reading will help you police the speed of your reading. If reading much faster than your normal academic pace causes you to miss important memory cues or main ideas, you will need to slow down. In reading situations where you are familiar with what you are reading, or the concepts are easy to understand it makes sense to increase your speed.

The final phase of your Task Management schedule, which has reserved time for a systematic review after completion of initial learning, is an excellent time for rapid reading. Rapid reading used as a review process reinforces prior exposure to content.

Normal Academic Reading Pace

Most of your reading will involve your normal academic reading rate. This speed of reading, as stated earlier, should be the fastest rate that allows you to have a high level of comprehension. The faster you can read, understand, and retain what you read, the easier your task of academic reading.

Intense Reading

There will be times when the complexity or difficulty of the material requires you to read slowly to comprehend. For example, if you are reading detailed technical content, chemistry equations, or abstract ideas, it may be necessary for you to read very slowly, perhaps to think about each sentence, even each word to obtain the level of desired understanding. The key to retention of what you learn with intensive reading is that after you complete a paragraph, you go back and reread the whole section at your regular academic pace. The practice of rereading complex content will help you understand how different ideas and concepts relate to each other, which will increase your retention of the material.

Discussion Questions:

How would you describe your speed of reading?

What kinds of material do you read for pleasure?

How does reading pleasure material differ from reading academic content?

Do you have the habit of reading at the same rate of speed that you talk?

Have you tried to increase your reading speed? If so, how?

NOTES

Lesson: Classroom Skills

How you spend your time before, during, and after class will determine how much you learn. Being an active versus passive consumer will enable you to benefit more from time spent in class. Your ability to understand and recall information presented in class dramatically improves your chances of getting good grades.

You will find some of your teachers enjoyable and easy to learn from because of their ability to lecture and organize class time. Your best teachers will grab your attention and stimulate your higher-order thinking skills and help you integrate new information and ideas into what you already know.

The reality is you will have some teachers, hopefully only a few, that will not make learning fun, and with whom you have to fight boredom. Your skills as a student will be more critical with these teachers. Regardless of the quality of teaching you experience, you should always consider yourself the primary agent in charge of learning and earning better grades.

Method: Consider Class Attendance a Must-Do Activity

Class Attendance Is A Major Predictor Of Academic Success

In high school, classes attendance is mandatory. In College, you may not have to go to class if you do not want to. Some professors have an attendance policy and use a sign-in procedure; many do not. The belief at the college level is you are an adult who has the freedom to decide whether or not you attend class. Missing what your professor emphasizes in a lecture puts you at a disadvantage with the next exam. Using a classmate's notes is not as effective as being present in class. To make up for a missed class, you will have to spend more time and effort than it would have taken to attend class.

Method: Develop A Positive Attitude Toward Class

Your attitude toward a class is directly related to how you think. Be mindful; take ownership of your thoughts about a course. If you allow yourself to cultivate a negative attitude toward a course with negative thoughts, it will be challenging to engage in behaviors you need to reach your goal of earning a better grade. Instead of complaining to yourself or others about the course, look for positives to cultivate a more accepting attitude. Promoting positive thoughts and blocking negative feelings will give you more energy to do what is needed to earn a better grade.

You Can Learn More In Less Time If You Prepare For Class

If you prepare for class, you can maximize your understanding and, more efficiently, develop the long-term memory you will need to be ready for exams. Preparation for a class is consistent with the
Survey step of the powerful SIR memory approach taught in the Memory Lesson.

Survey - Tell yourself in advance what it is you want to learn
             (Create Memory Cues)

Input

Reinforce

Often a teacher's class presentation follows the course textbook. If you use the strategic process of reading or previewing the chapter before it is covered in class, the teacher's presentation becomes your second exposure to the material. The class will function as a clarification and review. Using the class to reinforce the content, you have already introduced yourself to provides for a timely repetition that will help you more efficiently transfer content into your long-term memory and reduce the overall time and effort needed for study.

In courses that present complex and challenging content, prior reading can significantly increase understanding and performance. If, for example, your math or science instructor will be teaching complex content that comes directly from the text, reading a few pages ahead before class will help you to understand the teacher's lesson with much more clarity. You will find that concepts that were difficult to understand in class become easier to understand.

If you do not find the time to read in advance, previewing can also be a useful aid to building memory. Your preview can be as simple as reading the Table of Contents for the chapter. If a chapter summary is available, read the summary before you go to class. Take a few minutes to look over any discussion questions and visual aids provided with the chapter.

Method: Be An Active Learner
Be An Active Listener

Being physically present in class does not mean you are paying attention. Getting the most from the time you spend in classes can reduce the time needed for study outside of classes. Being an active participant in class starts with the intent to focus and get everything possible from the time you spend in class. It takes determination to both hear and try to understand what your teacher is saying.

You can think three or four times faster than your teacher can speak. Use this differential not to drift off, but rather to interpret and strive for understanding of the content. Maintain an alert body posture and consciously check and periodically recheck your level of concentration. Choose a seat in the front half or center of the room that will aid your focus, avoid sitting in sections that have distractions. Divide your eye contact between looking at your teacher, any supporting visuals, and your note-taking. If you participate in class discussions, ask and answer questions when the opportunity arises, it will aid your concentration and help you stay engaged during class time.

Being an Active Learner and Listener is consistent with the **Input** step of the SIR memory approach.

Survey

Input - Be an active learner (Learn with Concentration)

Reinforce

Not Enough To Just Be In Class ----- Be An Active Listener

Method: Review What You Learned In Class

Most Forgetting Occurs Soon After Initial Exposure
Unless You Reinforce Learning with
Recall and Repetition

To get the most from what you learn in class, you will want to use reinforcement procedures. Time of Reinforcement is an important factor in reducing the amount you forget. A timely review of new material will help you better remember at a later time.

In the lesson on Note-Taking, you will be encouraged to clarify and review your class notes the same day you created the notes. The longer you delay this clarification and review, the less beneficial the notes will be to you. A good habit is to use the time between classes or some of your reserved study block time each day to review class notes. If you did not read the textbook chapter section that corresponds to the recent class lecture before class, it is best to read it soon after the class.

Reviewing what you learned in class is consistent with the **Reinforce** step of the SIR memory approach.

Survey

Input

Reinforce - Ask yourself what you just learned (Practice Recall Using Memory Cues)

Method: Get To Know Your Teacher
Take Advantage Of Extra Help Offered

If you develop an interest in your teachers as people, it will be easier to have a positive attitude toward listening to them in class. Teachers sometimes reward effort, as well as specific accomplishments. If your teacher knows you, they will be more likely to notice your effort.

Often college teachers announce times when they are available to meet with students outside of regular class time. Make use of these teacher office hours to get extra help if needed or to clarify your performance on exams. In College, your professors often have graduate student assistants they can assign to you for individual tutoring.

Method: View All Opportunities For Extra Credit As Mandatory

If your teacher provides you with an opportunity for extra credit, you should view this as a mandatory assignment. Extra credit adds points that can make a difference in your final grade. Teachers have discretion in determining your final grade and will be much more likely to award a higher grade if you have taken advantage of extra credit opportunities.

Discussion Questions:

Do you prepare before you go to class? If so, how?

What actions help you concentrate in class?

What do you consider an ok reason for missing class?

How do you motivate yourself in the classes you like the least?

Do you try to control your attitude toward teachers or academic subjects?

Do you read textbook segments that correspond to class lectures before or after the content is presented in class? Why?

When do you clarify and review the notes you take in class?

NOTES

Lesson: Note - Taking

Good note-taking practices will enable you to study more effectively. Having quality notes to study from makes the goal of earning better grades easier. The content of this lesson can increase your ability to create notes and will make suggestions for the most effective ways to make use of your notes.

Teachers typically speak at a rate much faster than you can record what they are saying. The goal of note-taking is not to capture every word but rather to understand and condense the meaning of the lecture content in your own words. Your notes serve to store your understanding for future reference and study. It is helpful to understand that learning occurs during both the production and review of notes. The process of recording notes makes you focus and acts as a Repetition and Reinforcement that helps you transfer information from your short-term memory into the long-term memory. The memory cues you create when you are recording notes are crucial in helping you recall information later.

Qualities of Good Class Notes

- Your notes should provide an accurate and organized record of the content presented in class.
- Good notes make it easy for you to distinguish between main ideas and supporting information.
- To be the most useful, notes must compact content shared in class.
- If you paraphrase content, using your own words, you are interpreting information and will be better able to capture the meaning of what is shared.
- You want your notes to provide triggers or memory cues that help you recall both the primary meaning and necessary details.

Improve Your Note-Taking Skills

Where To Record Your Notes

Method: Use of Notebooks Versus A Laptop

The first step in note-taking is the selection of what you will use to record your notes. Although the opportunity might exist, research does not support you use a laptop. Although you might be able to type faster than you can write and have more notes, the process of typing interferes with the cognitive steps that transfer information from short-term to long-term memory. Making your notes by hand with a pen and paper is a slower process that requires you to listen, digest, and summarize before you record what you are hearing or seeing. Typing promotes a focus on the recording process at the expense of the understanding and summarizing process. When you take notes with pen and paper, you have the opportunity to apply strategies for linking ideas and creating memory cues that are not as easy to use with typing.

If you choose to use a laptop for initial note-taking, a review of your notes soon after you take them becomes more critical to maximize the value of the notes. Leave lots of space when you type so you can add handwritten notes that clarify ideas you have recorded. You will want to practice the habit of adding handwritten additions that take advantage of the memory cue and memory linkage steps presented in this lesson.

Method: Use a full-Size Spiral Notebook or Three-Ring Binder

It is recommended that you dedicate a separate notebook to each course you are taking. Using different color notebooks will make it easy for you to distinguish among classes. Avoid the use of small notebooks. Make use of full size 8 ½ by 11inch notebooks that open right to left. The full-size notebook will provide you with a better visual templet with which to connect ideas.

The benefit of spiral notebooks is their durability and the fact that you are not likely to lose pages. If you use a spiral notebook, try to use one that has pockets to store course information like the course syllabus or handouts. Always use notebooks that open right to left; avoid top to bottom style notebooks.

The benefit of using three-ring binders is the ability to insert pages. A three-hole punch enables you to add your course syllabus or other teacher handouts. You can add reading notes, notes that you choose to rewrite or test preparation steps like essay outlines for anticipated questions. When you are studying for an exam, you can shuffle the note pages to help develop memory linkages from multiple directions.

Hints For The Process of Note Taking

Method: Use Ink When There is No Need to Erase

When there is no need to erase, black or blue ink is preferable over pencil because it provides a sharper contrast that will help your visual image of the notes.

Method: When Taking Notes Use Right Hand Page Only

Make use of only the right-side page when recording class notes. Leave the left-hand page blank for possible use in your study process. The left-hand page, for example, could be used for creating a cognitive map of notes (mapping technique) based on what appears on the right-side page. You might use the left page for adding notes from your reading that clarify your class notes. If you believe it necessary to recopy your class notes, keep the original notes that may contain memory cues, and use the left page for the new notes.

If you are left-handed and want to use a spiral notebook, do consider purchasing spiral notebooks that have the spiral on the right side to avoid having your left hand resting on the spiral when writing. A search online will demonstrate ways you can flip your standard notebook pages so that you can work with the spiral on the right. When taking notes, you would use only the left page and leave the right side for clarification and study purposes.

Method: Keep Your Notes Organized

Stay organized by dating your notes and listing a topic title or chapter title at the start of each day's notes. Save, date, and coordinate handouts provided so they can be easily used to augment your notes when studying. Number the loose-leaf sheets if you are using a three-ring binder.

Method: Skip Spaces Between Ideas

Do not attempt to record notes in an outline form unless the teacher is providing the outline. A more effective method is to leave spaces between ideas or concepts. You should skip larger spaces when you go from one major topic to another.

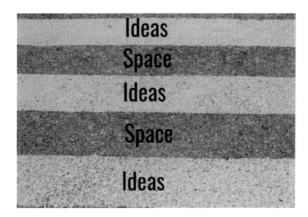

Method: Develop and Use Abbreviations and Acronyms When Taking Notes

The use of abbreviations and acronyms is a convenient way to be able to record notes quickly. Not having to write out words or phrases frees up our mind to process the meaning of what you are hearing. The more shorthand techniques you use, the more time you will have for thinking and taking additional notes.

Become familiar with commonly used abbreviations and acronyms and be creative in making your own. An abbreviation is a shortened form of a word; you can use acronyms as a form of abbreviation for a series of words. When you create abbreviations or acronyms, it is a good idea to make a legend at the top of your note page until you become thoroughly familiar with the shortcut.

Examples of commonly used abbreviations
& = and
W = with
W/O = without
b/c = because
b/4 = before
ea. = each
e.g. = for example
i.e., =in other words
impt = important
ex =example

Shorten Form of Words/subjects
Psy = Psychology
Hist = History
Chem= Chemistry
Eng = English
Bio =Biology
Span = Spanish

Acronyms
NATO = North Atlantic Treaty Organization
DNC=Democratic National Committee
RNC = Republican National Committee
USA = United States of America
ASAP = as soon as possible
AKA = also known as
Circa (CA) =around the time

How To Make Use Of Your Notes

Method: Read and Clarify Your Class Notes the Same Day You Take Them

Forgetting often occurs soon after learning unless there is Reinforcement. Reviewing and clarifying your class notes soon after making them serve to solidify the link between your notes and the body of information they represent. If you put down your notes for days without first reviewing them, you will lose many memory associations.

Method: Review Your Notes Often

Repetition is a key method for remembering. If you take the time to read over your notes often, the task of being ready for an exam will be much easier. Each time you review your class notes or review what you have read in your text, the memory cue associations become stronger. The second and subsequent reviews become more comfortable and faster.

In College, you will often have gaps of time between classes. Using the time before, between, or right after classes for reviewing and clarifying class notes is a great way to reduce the overall amount of time you have to study to be ready for exams. Spend the first portion of your evening study block reviewing your notes if you have not had the opportunity to review your notes earlier in the day.

Clarify and Review Your Notes The Same Day You Record Them
Review Your Notes Often

Method: Learn and Make Use of the Alternative Formats of Note-Taking

Formats Of Note-Taking

Traditional or Linear Notes - Record Using the Order of Presentation
Cornell Method - Uses A Memory Column
Mapping Technique - A Graphic Method, Uses Diagrams

You can make your notes using a variety of formats. Notes are personal; any note-taking methods that aid in the learning process can be useful. You will want to choose your style of note-taking based on what you believe is the most effective, given the learning situation. You are not limited to picking and sticking to a single method of note-taking; you could make use of the Linear outline method, the Cornell Method, or Mapping Techniques all in the same lecture presentation.

Traditional or Linear Note-Taking

Recording notes in the order in which the instructor presents them is a traditional technique for making notes. The process should make use of a hierarchal process that facilitates the separation of central topics from supporting information. One approach is to place major headings or concepts to the left and indent the supporting information to the right. Leave open space between lines to separate ideas and to be able to add notes later. Although labeling is not required, you can use a system of labeling the indentations using bullets, numbers, or letters. When you review your notes, you can treat the main headings as questions and use them as memory cues.

Cornell Method of Note-Taking

The Cornell Method enables you to organize and quickly make connections between ideas by using two columns with one containing a keyword that serves as a memory cue, the other holding your notes that elaborate on the keyword. The Cornell Method is appealing because of the ease it provides for practicing memory recall and facilitating multiple repetitions. You build memory by covering the right side of the page and using the cue word in the left column as a stimulus for recalling what you have hidden. You can write the memory cue words when you are initially taking notes or when you are reviewing and clarifying your notes.

To set-up, the method, draw a line vertically down your 8 ½ X 11 inch note page approximately six inches from the right edge. The right column created provides you with space for writing. Use the left column for cue words (prompt words) that will stimulate you to recall the ideas recorded in the note section. In a reserved bottom space, you can record possible exam questions during or soon after class when the content the teacher emphasizes is fresh in your mind.

Mapping Techniques for Note-Taking

Mapping is a graphic method that uses diagrams to organize and link ideas together. The process of mapping uses logical learning with visual learning. As you make notes with this method, you use your critical thinking skills to organize main themes, supporting facts, and ideas in a visual format. Keywords or briefly stated concepts are connected by arrows to create a logical sequence of information. Mapping helps you develop linkage among keywords that serve as memory cues.

The benefit of the mapping method is that more of your mental focus is on understanding and condensing material into keywords or short concepts and less on the production of notes. You save time and mental energy by being less wordy. When you study from mapping notes, you let your brain add context to the keywords or short concepts you recorded. This thinking process helps transfer knowledge from short-term to long-term memory.

When you review notes made in the Linear or Cornell method, it is a useful exercise to condense notes by creating a mapping version of notes on the previously blank left-hand page. The format of mapping makes it easy to add new notes to existing notes. You can easily blend reading notes into classroom notes by adding or expanding connecting keywords.

Try Different Approaches of Note-taking

Traditional or Linear Notes

Cornell Method

Mapping Technique

Example of Linear Notes

History of Americas

Date: _____

European Colonization

<u>Spain</u> colonized (COL) SW US, Florida + Caribbean

<u>Portugal</u> COL Brazil

<u>England</u> COL East Coast US, North Pacific Coast + most Canada

<u>France</u> COL Quebec, Central US + parts of Eastern Canada

<u>Aside</u> Top World Languages of 2010

#1	Chinese	955 million
#2	Spanish	405 million
#3	English	360 million
#4	Hindi	310 million
#5	Arabic	295 million
#6	Portuguese	215 million

Example of Cornell Method of Note-Taking

History of Americas

Date: _____

European Colonization

Colonies?	COL = Colonized
Spain	Spain COL SW US, Florida + Caribbean
Portugal	Portugal COL Brazil
England	England COL East Coast US, North Pacific Coast, Most Canada
France	France COL Quebec, Central US + Parts Eastern Canada

Current Top Languages

World Languages (2010)

#		
#1	Chinese	955 million
#2	Spanish	405 million
#3	English	360 million
#4	Hindi	310 million
#5	Arabic	295 million
#6	Portuguese	215 million

Possible test Question: Know US Colony areas settled by each European country

Example of Mapping Technique for Note-Taking

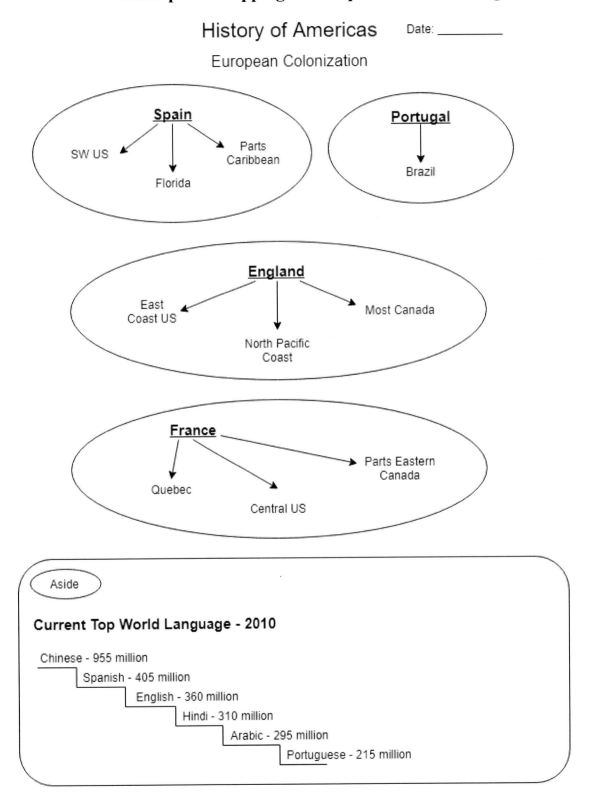

History of Americas

Date: _____

European Colonization

Spain
SW US
Florida
Parts Caribbean

Portugal
Brazil

England
East Coast US
North Pacific Coast
Most Canada

France
Quebec
Central US
Parts Eastern Canada

Aside

Current Top World Language - 2010

Chinese - 955 million
Spanish - 405 million
English - 360 million
Hindi - 310 million
Arabic - 295 million
Portuguese - 215 million

Note-Taking Outside of Class

Method: Notes for Papers and Projects

If you are collecting information from multiple sources like articles or supplemental reference books when writing a paper or preparing for a presentation keeping notes is essential. The use of 5 X 8 index cards is an excellent tool for this kind of note-taking. Save time by recording your reference source in the format that you will use for your reference list.

Method: Notes Embedded in Textbook

If you are reading from a text that you own and can mark up, you can apply note-taking strategies as part of your approach to reading. Your highlights or annotations in the text should focus on creating memory cues that will help you recall what you have read. Most textbooks help you capture central concepts by providing headings, subheadings, and other memory aids like discussion questions, chapter introductions, and chapter summaries. You can add to these memory cues by selectively highlighting or by underlying keywords or phrases and by writing questions, thoughts, reactions, main ideas, or summary statements in the margins. If you come across an unfamiliar word or a word you do not understand, have a system such as drawing a box around the word, which will remind you to go back and search for clarity. Multiple choice questions often use these unfamiliar words.

Method: Creating Notes from Textbook

Consider making written notes from reading to give yourself an opportunity for repetition and reinforcement. A simple, fast approach for creating reading notes is to use the Linear approach of copying textbook headings and subheadings, leaving blank space for inserting notes. If you use a mapping approach, make diagrams using abbreviated textbook headings and subheadings. Complete your mapping diagram by adding keywords and key concepts taken from your reading.

Discussion Questions

What kind of notebook do you prefer for recording class notes? Why?

Describe your approach to creating class notes as you listen in class.

What methods do you use to clarify and correct class notes?

When do you typically first read the notes you have recorded in class? Why?

Describe the research notes you create when preparing for a term paper.

How might your style of note-taking differ with History, Math, or Foreign Language courses?

Have you ever used a mapping (graphic) approach when recording notes?

How and when do you review study your class notes? Why?

NOTES

Lesson: Memory Skills Part II

More Strategies To Build Memory

The <u>Memory Skills Part I</u> lesson provided methods that made use of logical connections and links to build long-term memory. The **S**urvey, **I**nput, **R**einforcement (**SIR**) memory step approach takes advantage of linkage and the association of ideas to create a memory. However, much of what you have to learn as a student is factual, and you will not be able to build new memory through association with what you already know.

There will be learning tasks where the easiest and often the only way to make information part of your long-term memory is through memorization. Rote memorization is a learning process based on repetition. You will be better able to remember and use the information, the more you repeat it. This lesson will share strategies that will make your repetitions more effective.

Mnemonic devices are tricks or gimmicks that help you remember. This lesson will present multiple Mnemonic tools that are effective and fun to use. Chances are you know and already use mnemonic tricks to retain information. Teachers often share mnemonic devices that help with the subject they are teaching. Mnemonics are a simple way of building memory using made-up associations that help you recall more easily. Often these made-up associations have no logical link to the material you are recalling. To work, you must accurately remember the made-up memory cue that serves as an anchor to the content you seek to retain. In addition to learning commonly established mnemonics, you will be encouraged to experiment with creating your own memory devices.

Repetition Is The Primary Strategy for Rote Memorization

Method: Use Rote Memorization When Necessary

You are encouraged to avoid memorization whenever possible and rely on association methods, but at times you must memorize. When you must rely on memorization, it is important to accept this fact and memorize what has to memorized as soon as possible.

The reason many students do not get good grades in math, science, foreign language, and other courses that require a base foundation of content is that they delay learning what has to be memorized. Your goal with memorization is to know facts automatically without having to think about it.

Examples of When Rote Memorization is Necessary:

Multiplication Tables
Can you remember when you learned the multiplication table when you were younger? Nine times seven equals__?__ is a simple example of a memory item that might best be acquired by using multiple repetitions, with a recall process until the answer sixty-three is automatic.

Spelling
Learning to spell words often requires memorization that comes from repetition.

Facts
There is "factual" information you need to know for everyday living, and to be able to best function in society and at work. Many academic subjects require you to learn facts as a foundation to progress in the discipline. You learn facts through exposure and repetition.

Language
Learning words, verbs, and clichés through multiple exposures and practicing repetitions is how we learn languages. For example, the verb "To Speak" in Spanish is **Hablar** or "To Speak" in Italian is **Parlare**, this knowledge can only be acquired by exposure and repetition.

Method: Multiple Repetitions and Recall

Repetition is required to memorize anything. The best way to make use of repetition is to create a stimulus or memory cue that you can use to practice recalling the information you want to remember. The use of index cards with the memory cue on one side and the factual information on the reverse side works well when employing the method of rote memorization. Using a time interval between repetitions will make the memory association stronger. Repetition over time is a powerful learning technique. Recalling before you go to sleep at night and then practicing recall the following morning is more useful for creating long-term memory than trying to build memory in just one study block.

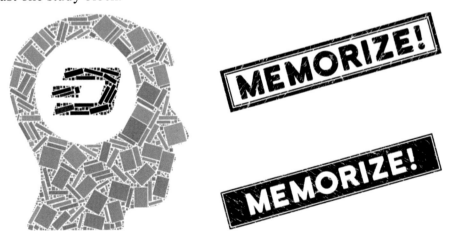

Recognize When Rote Memorization is Necessary

Method: Make Use of All of Your Learning Modalities

"See it," "Say it," "Hear it," and "Write It" when you are trying to build memory. Our modalities of learning, our senses, play a significant role in memory. You can increase your capacity to learn when you recognize and make use of multiple modalities.

Modalities of Learning

Visual Memory - The idiom "A picture is worth a thousand words" highlights the notion that "Seeing It" activates your visual memory. An image, even the image of a word or words, can help to both convey ideas and aid the memory process. To activate visual memory, you must focus on the image you are trying to remember. Another tool with visual memory is the use of color and color contrast.

If you find it easy to recognize people you have met before, chances are you have the habit of focusing on the details of their face or image. If you pay attention and try to "SEE" when you are using rote memory, fewer repetitions will be necessary.

Auditory Memory - To maximize your academic success, you must rely a great deal on auditory memory. You will benefit more from class lectures if you listen intently, analyze what you hear, and store the information in your memory. Speaking, the process of saying out loud uses both auditory memory and your kinesthetic or motor memory. When you are trying to use rote memory to learn something, the process of "Saying it" and "Hearing it" can help you build long-term memory.

Motor (kinesthetic) Memory - You can learn by doing. In sports, we take it for granted that the act of doing is a learning process; we call it practice. When attempting to learn material using Rote Memorization, the process of writing can help build memory. You may recall in elementary school when you were asked to write the words you were trying to learn ten times. The exercise helped you build memory both by repetition but also by the practice of doing.

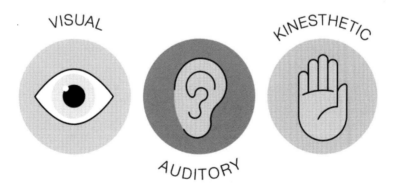

Use Multiple Modalities to Learn

Method: Use Associations to Build Memory

Associate new information with existing information
Categories of Associations

Similarity - This is a process in which you take the new information you want to learn and associate it with existing knowledge. For example, you might remember the name of a person you are just meeting by associating him/her with a person you know who has the same name.

Contrast - When using the contrast method to develop memory associations, you note how things are different. If you are trying to learn the states on the east coast of the United States, you might note Maine is the farthest north as opposed to Florida, which is the most southern. You might also note Maine as having a cold climate as opposed to Florida having a warm climate.

Matched-Pairs - You can probably think of items we commonly associate with others like hammer and nail, and bread and butter. The method of building matched pairs can be useful in academics. You might, for example, match Presidents with significant historical events like Lincoln with the Civil War or Franklin Roosevelt with World War II.

Method: Make Use of Acrostics as a Mnemonic Tool

An acrostic is a fabricated sentence where the first letter of each word serves as a memory cue for something you want to remember.

Academic Subject Examples:

ASTRONOMY- Order of Planets, Pluto No Longer Considered a Planet
My Very Educated Mother Just Said Uh-oh! No Pluto
Mercury, Venus, Earth, Mars, Jupiter, Saturn, Uranus, Neptune, Pluto

CHEMISTRY-Series of Alkanes
My Enormous Pig Bounces Pretty High
Methane, Ethane, Propane, Butane, Pentane, Hexane

MATHEMATICS-Order of Operations
Please Excuse My Dear Aunt Sally
Parentheses, Exponents, Multiplication, Division, Addition, Subtraction

MUSIC-Treble Clef (Musical Scales)
Every Good Boy Deserves, Fudge

Method: Make Use of Acronyms as a Mnemonic Tool

An acronym is when you recall a word using letters from another word.

Examples of acronyms:

HOMES (to remember the names of the great lakes)
Huron, Ontario, Michigan, Erie, and Superior

Roy G BIV (Colors of the Rainbow)
Red, Orange, Yellow, Green, Blue, Indigo, and Violet

SPA (Order in which the great Greek philosophers lived)
Socrates, Plato, Aristotle

AIM (Major cultures in Mesoamerica and Latin America)
Aztec, Inca, Maya

Pvt. Tim Hall (for the essential amino acids)
Phenylalanine, Valine, Threonine, Tryptophan, Isoleucine, Methionine, Histidine, Arginine, Leucine, Lysine

BRAT (Diet for an upset stomach)
Bananas, Rice, Applesauce, Toast

Acronym: BRAT (Diet for an upset stomach)
Bananas, Rice, Applesauce, Toast

Method: Make Use of Rhymes as a Mnemonic Tool

Rhymes use sounds and the connections of words to help you remember.

Rhymes-Jack and Jill, Baa Baa Black Sheep and Twinkle Twinkle Little Star are examples of nursery rhymes you probably have as part of your memory.

Examples of Rhyme use to remember facts:

How Many Days in a Month?
> "Thirty days hath September, April, June, and November; All the rest have thirty-one Excepting February alone: Which has twenty-eight, that's fine, Till leap year gives it twenty-nine."

When did Columbus sail to America?
> "In fourteen hundred and ninety-two, Columbus sailed the Ocean Blue."

Rhyme for remembering spelling:
> "I before E except after C, and when sounding like "ay" as in Neighbor or Weigh."

> Rhyme: for spelling Mississippi "M...I...SS...I...SS...I...PP...I"

Rhyme for predicting the next day's weather:
> "Red sky at night, sailor's delight, red sky in the morning, sailors take warning."

Rhyme to learn the rules of multiplying negative numbers:
> "Minus times minus is a plus. The reason for this we need not discuss."

Method: Make Use of Spelling Mnemonics

Gimmicks, you can use to remember the correct spelling of words.

Examples of Spelling Mnemonics:

ARITHMETIC:
> A Rat In The House May Eat The Ice Cream

RHYTHM:
> Rhythm Helps Your Two Hips Move

Potassium:
> One Tea two sugars –The correct spelling has One T and Two Ss

Principal:
> Proper use - The Principal is a "pal" of mine

Method: Make Use of Link Method Mnemonics

Uses the process of making associations between things

You can use this method in the study of foreign languages.

Italian example:
> Hand in Italian is "Mano"
> Imagine a man washing his hands

Spanish examples:
> Rice in Spanish is "Arroz"
> Imagine shooting arrows at a plate of rice

> Cow in Spanish is "vaca"
> Imagine a cow using a vacuum cleaner

Discussion Questions:

What are some of the memory tricks or gimmicks that you use to recall information?

What strategies did you use as a child to learn the multiplication tables?

When you meet a new person, what methods do you use to remember their name?

Do you learn better with visual or auditory stimulation?

The acronym BRAT is used by physicians to help patients deal with an upset stomach. What do the letters BRAT stand for?

How would you use the acrostic tool "Please Excuse My Dear Aunt Sally."

How do you remember how many days are in each month?

Do you have any memory tricks you created that you can share?

NOTES

Lesson: Papers, Projects And Class Presentations

Set Specific Goals And Timelines

One of the noteworthy differences between High School academics and College academics is the number of papers, projects, and class presentations required. These assignments will determine a significant portion of the grade you receive in a course.

Often professors are generous with deadlines allowing you until the last several weeks of the semester to complete these assignments. If you procrastinate, there is a strong possibility that the projects will interfere with your exam preparation time. The quality of any writing assignment, class project, or class presentation will be hurt or helped based on the amount of time you have allocated to complete the task.

This lesson will provide you with guidance on the steps recommended for the completion of these types of assignments. You will experience more comfort, less anxiety, and a higher level of success if you plan and set specific goals and timelines for completion of steps that lead to finishing each assignment.

College Writing

Your ability to be a competent, skilled writer will serve you both in your academic courses and throughout your career. When you graduate from college and are seeking employment, it will be common to see job announcements that are looking for candidates that have "excellent oral and written communications." In addition to the expectation of quality writing in all courses, many colleges now have the requirement that students complete a minimum number of "writing intensive" courses.

Colleges understand that you may be starting your studies needing a lot of work to improve your writing skills. As a first-year college student, you are likely to have an English composition course to help you develop your writing skills. Most English Composition Professors are dedicated and talented at improving writing skills. The task of improving your writing ability may seem difficult, but you can do it, and the rewards are great. Starting with a positive attitude and accepting the need to improve your writing abilities is an essential first step. Many colleges have Writing Centers and Writing Tutors available if you need extra help. When you are required to complete a writing assignment, make it a personal goal to be a better writer, not just to get the task done.

Method: Familiarize Yourself with Library Resources and Make Use of Library Support Services

Most colleges have either face-to-face library orientations or online virtual orientation tours. You should complete a library orientation in the first few weeks that you are on campus, which will help you understand how easy it is to get started with your paper or presentation requirements. Librarians are helpful professionals who can guide you on how to locate the resources you need, but the expectation is that you will have first completed a library orientation. Familiarity with library resources can make the completion of your paper or project an easier task. Do not assume that research consists of simple online Google-type searches. Most academic areas have specialized databases and search engines that you will need to be familiar with to gather acceptable references. Colleges pay a license fee that allows their students to have access to many academic resources. After you complete the orientation, you will know what is available and how best to access the resources.

Method: Learn to Use MLA, APA or Other Required Style Formatting

When you write your research papers or hand in any formal academic paper, you will most likely be required to use a specific format. The most common formats are those developed by the MLA (Modern Language Association) and the APA (American Psychological Association.) You will be required to use a specific format for citations listed in your reference bibliography. A great time-saver is to record the citation of each reference you use in the correct format so that when it comes time to write your paper, the task will be easier. If you record citations on your computer, it will be a simple cut and paste process to complete the bibliography. Required MLA format includes paper size, margins, text formatting, headings, page numbers, and citations. APA format is different than the MLA format and is a common requirement in your psychology or social science classes.

Method: Understand and Avoid Plagiarism

If you use another author's words or ideas and present them as your own, it is plagiarism. You must give the writer of your source proper credit in the form of a citation. Using a citation is not enough; you must use a paraphrase in your own words or put the material in a quotation format. Include a citation if you are unsure about whether it is necessary to provide a citation or not.

A common practice of your English composition professors and other professors is to require that you email papers or submit them in an electronic format. Computer programs are used that scan student writing and identify possible plagiarism. If you provide your paper in standard paper format, your professors are adept at recognizing plagiarism and, if in doubt, can require an electronic version to complete a plagiarism scan. Do not make the mistake of making use of offers online that sell term papers; such use is an offense that could lead to severe consequences, even expulsion from your college.

Method: Budget Adequate Time with a Spaced Learning Approach

Papers, Projects, and Class Presentations have deadlines. If you have the opportunity to select your date of presentation, try to choose a time that does not compete with your review time for exams. When you present early in the semester, you will be free to spend more time on other assignments and preparing for exams. Class presentations are often group projects with each student presenting a portion of the presentation. You may need to be assertive with other group members and convince them that it is a good idea to get an early presentation date.

The amount of time it will take for you to complete a paper will vary depending on the assignment requirement. If research is required, it will take longer than if you are writing a reaction to something or presenting ideas based on the knowledge you already have. No matter how simple or challenging you judge a writing assignment to be, it is a good idea to give yourself an abundance of time to complete the project. You should consider it self-defeating to procrastinate and wait until just a few days before the assignment is due.

As a rule, if you are writing a short theme paper (1-4 pages) allow at a minimum of four to six days. Give yourself a minimum of six to ten days if the assignment is a longer paper (5-10 pages or more.) Research papers require more time than theme papers and typically take five or more weeks for completion. All papers benefit from a time lag between completion of the first draft and the final review and revision. The time lag gives you more perspective on the quality of what you are writing. You will want to create a schedule that budgets time and sets deadlines for completion of each step of the writing process.

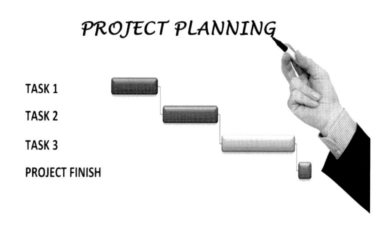

Complete Your Writing Assignment in Steps

Method: Complete Your Writing Assignment in Steps

Whether you have a short theme paper or more extensive research paper, completion of the task will be easier if you divide it into steps. Having a target time for finishing each step will ease your stress and give you adequate time to write the best paper possible.

Step 1 Select the Topic

Set a goal of choosing at least a tentative topic or thesis within a few days of receiving the assignment. Many students delay starting work on the task because they do not commit to a topic. When possible, choose a subject you have an interest in and would like to learn more about and express your views. If you enjoy the topic, you will be more motivated to work on the assignment.

Step 2 Explore Resources Needed

If you have the information you need to begin writing readily available, you are more likely to work on the paper. Set an early deadline for exploring and acquiring the necessary resources to write your paper. A review of resources will help you decide if you need to adjust or select another topic. If the topics you have to choose from are also available to classmates, being proactive in signing out book resources gives you a definite advantage.

Step 3 Create Notes from the Resources

Create a target time goal for gathering notes from your resources. If you use 5 X 8 index cards, you will have the flexibility to organize and keep track of your sources. Write your notes as a paraphrase or be sure to use quotation marks if copying directly from the resource to avoid issues later with plagiarism. On the index cards carefully record the citation you will need in the bibliography of your paper; be sure to record the page numbers from which you got the information.

Step 4 Outline what you are Going to Write

Set a deadline for the creation of an outline that you will use when writing the paper. Carefully review the instructions for the assignment before you start. Take a moment to reflect on the purpose your teacher has for the paper. Do the instructions call for you just to share information gathered or to form a thesis to be discussed and supported? Does the teacher want you to analyze, compare, interpret, or react to the information? A lot of the time, teachers are looking for your critical thinking skills displayed in the paper.

Review your resource notes and use them to guide the creation of your outline. Allow time to think about the information you have gathered, play with ideas in your mind, brainstorm ways you might organize the paper. The outline is a guide that you can add to or delete from as you write.

Step 5 Write the first draft

Set a realistic time goal for the completion of the first draft of your paper. Your first draft should not be your last draft. Recognize that you are completing both the process of expressing ideas and the mechanics of writing. You do not have to start your paper from the beginning; some accomplished writers begin with the body of the paper and add the introduction and conclusion later. The first draft is a rough draft, so you can let the ideas flow freely, knowing you will have the opportunity to reorganize what you write. The cut and paste functions of word processing programs are a convenient way to move around ideas in your paper.

Step 6 Prepare the final paper

Give yourself time so that you have at least a day between your rough draft and preparation of the final paper. This time-lapse will help with your objectivity and inspire changes that make the paper better. Spend time focusing on sentence structure, the transition of ideas, grammar, spelling, word choice, and punctuation. Your final paper should be error-free and conform to the format required, whether it be MLA, APA, or any other format in the paper directions.

Discussion Questions:

Describe the largest writing assignment you were required to complete in high school. What do you remember most about the challenges of completing the assignment?

Describe how you would go about completing a 6-10 page reaction paper to a novel you are required to read?

Do you have a habit of completing the work needed to finish papers and projects early, or do you tend to procrastinate?

When given a choice of time for presenting a class project, what are your goals for the time selected?

What do you like most and like least when required to be part of a group project and class presentation?

NOTES

Lesson: Controlling Test Anxiety

Perform At Your Highest Level

Whenever there is a demand to perform, some anxiety is common and natural. There is, however, a difference between being a little nervous because you want to do well and having your stress interfere with your ability to show what you have learned. The methods in this lesson will help you control and reduce anxiety, so it does not interfere with your test performance.

Why do you study? For most students, the desire for success and the fear of failure are both motivating factors. Using the fear of doing poorly to motivate yourself to study is ok in moderation. However, using fear as a motivator needs to be controlled to the degree that it does not harm your ability to perform.

Method: Adequately Prepare for Exams

The amount of performance anxiety you experience will correspond to the level of confidence you have in your preparation. If you believe your study efforts have been adequate, you will have confidence in your ability to perform on a test. Of course, you can always study more, but you will want to become comfortable with what you believe is a reasonable level of study. Confidence in your preparation will be easier to obtain if you have used the spaced learning and time management methods recommended in this program. The use of adequate time to allow for learning in smaller chunks and the practice of spaced reinforcement using repetition and recall builds confidence. If you rely on a cramming approach for your preparation, it will be harder to justify a high level of confidence.

You Do Not Have to Be Perfect to Be Good

If you tend to be a perfectionist, it essential to remind yourself that "you do not have to be perfect to be good." Aim high but do not demand perfection. No one test answer or single test is going to determine your future. If you fall short of your goal for success on a given test, you will want to learn from that experience and adjust your strategies for achieving success.

Method: Manage Your Time The Night Before An Exam

You will want to avoid cramming the night before an exam. Cramming is better than no exposure but a poor substitution for proper preparation. If you have used a spaced learning approach with systematic reinforcement over time, you will be much better prepared for the exam than students trying to learn material for the first time. If you attempt to cover or relearn too much information in a short period, your memory associations could get mixed up and confused, which will hurt performance. The best approach is to complete a systematic review process that relies on reinforcing the memory cues and memory associations you have already established in your spaced learning preparation process.

Method: Manage Your Physical State Before the Exam

Your memory will serve you best when you are not exhausted. Avoid arriving at the exam without having had proper rest. As a general rule, do not get less than one hour of your usual amount of sleep. If you need more time for your preparation, it is better to get to sleep at a reasonable time and get up an hour earlier to complete your exam review. Proper nutrition is also important before an exam, make time to eat a regular or small meal before the exam, avoid eating a large meal that can make you sleepy. Excessively high levels of caffeine will increase your level of anxiety and harm your memory function.

Method: Use Constructive "Self-Talk" Before the Exam

Your feelings, which include fear or confidence, comes from your thoughts. Be careful; you can worry yourself into a state of high anxiety even when you are adequately prepared. Monitor what you are saying to yourself so that you do not create high-performance anxiety. Avoid making the irrational demand that you be "perfectly" ready for the exam. If you adhere to the irrational belief that you need to be perfect to be good, the resulting anxiety level could harm your performance. Convince yourself that although each exam is important, no one test is critical to your academic success. Obtaining good grades in most courses will allow you to earn a lower grade occasionally and still be considered an excellent student.

Use Constructive "Self-Talk"

Method: Avoid Cramming Just Before the Exam Starts

Cramming right before an exam increases the possibility of "Information Interference," a process where material recently focused on acts as a block to previously studied material. If you believe you need to study right before an exam, limit the scope of what you are reviewing to one or two small informational areas. If you have adequately prepared, attempts to review a lot of material the hour before the exam can do more harm than good. Last hour cramming can increase your anxiety level and therefore harm your ability to show what you know.

If possible, the hour before an exam, you should engage in activities that will lower your anxiety level. You might, for example, take a comfortable walk or socialize with friends that have a good sense of humor. Try to stay away from activities like talking to nervous friends who might increase your anxiety. You might find it comforting to carry your notebook and textbook but try not to use the books right before the exam unless essential. Arrive at the exam early and focus your thoughts on constructive self-talk and exam-taking strategies.

Method: How to Deal with Exam Panic

Take A Short Time-Out If You Are Experiencing Exam Panic

Exam panic is a condition that can arise when a high level of performance anxiety causes you to draw a blank when asked to answer questions you should know. The inability to answer causes you to develop an even higher level of performance anxiety. You will understand the phenomenon when you compare it to the last time you came across someone you previously met and whose name you should know, but you simply cannot recall their name. Minutes after the person leaves, you can remember the name.

If you experience exam panic, stop attempting to answer the questions and take a two-minute mental time out from the exam. Sit back in your chair and concentrate on breathing normally; a full breath in your nose followed by a full breath out your mouth. Think about something pleasant and relaxing. You might, for example, fantasize about winning a lottery or taking a dream vacation. This method is the mental equivalent of changing the television channel from a horror show to a relaxing show.

When the two minutes have passed, go back to the exam, and in your calmer state, assure yourself that you will simply do the best you can, and that will be good enough. Skip questions to which you don't know the answer and build your confidence by answering questions you do know. You can go back to the questions you skipped later when, in fact, your anxiety will be lower, and your ability to remember information better.

Method: Avoid Useless Stress During and After the Exam

The idiom "don't cry over spilled milk" applies here. You should go into an exam conscious of the fact that that you may not know the answer to every question. Stressing over, not knowing an answer serves no productive purpose during the exam and can raise your performance anxiety. After the test, take the attitude of the song "Don't Worry Be Happy" it serves no purpose to stress out over something that you cannot fix. If you are not happy with your exam results, promise yourself that you will use better strategies to prepare for the next exam.

Discussion Questions:

Describe a situation when the pressure to perform or to have an answer diminished your ability to respond.

Have you ever experienced exam panic, where a high level of anxiety caused you to draw a blank, a total inability to answer questions? Please describe the situation.

Do you tend to be a perfectionist; how do you think this affects your level of exam anxiety?

What was the most important test you ever had to complete? How did you control your anxiety with this test?

What do you believe is the best way to spend the hour just before a comprehensive exam?

What methods do you use to control the level of anxiety you have before an important exam?

NOTES

Lesson: Test-Taking Skills

Maximize Your Test Scores

Tests are intended to be a measure of how much you have learned. Regardless of how well you prepare and how much you know, your level of skill in the process of completing the test will factor into the grade you earn. To achieve the highest possible grades, in addition to thorough preparation, you will want to use the most effective skills and strategies for test-taking. This lesson will introduce you to general test-taking strategy as well as specific strategies for completing multiple-choice test questions, true/false questions, and essay questions.

GENERAL EXAM STRATEGIES

Method: Over Learn for Your First Exam

The first test with any teacher is the most challenging because you are unfamiliar with the teacher's style of giving exams. Approach the first test with the attitude that it is the most important test of the course. It will be helpful to set the goal of overlearning for the first exam. To overlearn requires you to increase repetitions and test your recall even after you think you have mastered the material. You want to be able to recall content quickly and easily. The grade you earn in the first test will set the standard for the final grade you will receive in the course. Getting off to a strong start by obtaining a good grade will foster a higher level of motivation and will keep your anxiety level low.

Method: Read and Understand Test Directions

The anxiety or excitement of getting started with an exam may cause you to jump into answering questions without first taking the time to read the test instructions carefully. Instructions are there for a purpose; do take the time to understand the test directions.

Last Minute Oral Exam Instructions

Pay attention to your teacher at the start of the exam. Valuable information regarding how to proceed with test questions may be given orally. It is not uncommon for your instructor to clarify or provide hints on how best to answer select test questions. These last-minute instructions often come from the teacher's observation of how students might misinterpret or respond incorrectly to questions.

Method: Memory Download

A memory download can be a useful strategy for some types of exams. You may find it helpful to review information like a math formula or the outline you prepared for an essay just before the start of an exam. The review of only a few facts before an exam begins is not the same as cramming, which can cause information interference and performance anxiety.

Memory download is a process of jotting down facts that are fresh in your mind for use as you complete the exam. A word of caution, be sure you complete this process in a way that it is clear to your teacher that what you jot down occurred after you put away all resources and after the exam has started.

Method: Preview the Exam Before You Start

You should preview the exam before you start. Understand the structure of the test; for example, the test might be half multiple-choice questions and half essay questions. Read the essay requirements before you start answering other questions. Knowledge of the essay questions will allow you to reflect on how you will respond, and better enable earlier parts of the exam to stimulate ideas. Being familiar with the essay questions will aid you in budgeting the time you have available to complete the test.

Method: Budget the Time You Have to Complete the Test

An important strategy when taking a test is to make optimal use of the time available. Allot time for completion of each portion of the test and time to review your answers. If, for example, you have a 45-minute class and the test consists of 30 multiple choice questions and two short essays, you might plan 20 minutes to complete the multiple-choice segment and 20 minutes to complete the essay segment. In the remaining 5 minutes, you can review answers or return to select multiple-choice questions.

When time is a factor, do not allow yourself to spend too much time on any one question. If a multiple-choice question requires extra time, note that question and return to it after you have answered the other more manageable questions. When you have essay requirements, pace yourself so that you have adequate time to complete your answers.

MULTIPLE-CHOICE QUESTIONS

Method: Apply Strategies for Multiple-Choice Questions

Multiple-choice questions test your ability to eliminate the wrong answer and recognize the right answer. If you apply the strategies listed below, when answering multiple-choice questions, it will increase the probability of selecting the correct answer.

Multiple Choice Question Strategy	In what year was The Missouri Compromise passed in Congress?
Try to answer the question without looking at alternatives	A B C D

Multiple Choice Question Strategy	In what year was The Missouri Compromise passed in Congress?
Read all alternatives Before making Your selection	A 1820 B 1812 C 1865 D 1917

Let's assume you believe the answer is 1820. Even though you think you know the answer, and your response is one of the alternatives, read the other options before you record your final choice. Reading other alternatives may serve to clarify the question and the accuracy of your answer. There is an added benefit to reading the different options. The wrong answers may help you with other questions on the exam. Can you associate events with the other dates listed in this question?

Multiple Choice Question Strategy	In what year was The Missouri Compromise passed in Congress?
View answer selection As a two way process Elimination and Selection	A 1820 B 1812 C 1865 X(Wrong time frame) D 1917 X(Wrong time frame)

Make it a practice to eliminate the two most likely wrong answers and then compare and select from the remaining responses. The correct answer is A, 1820.

Qualifier words affect the certainty and specificity of a statement

An essential strategy when answering multiple-choice questions is to identify qualifier words and phrases that appear in both the question and the alternative answers. Your skill in identifying and factoring in the impact of qualifier words will make a big difference in your level of achievement.

When you have **absolute qualifier words** such as **never, none, all, always, no,** or **entirely,** you need only **one exception** to change the correctness of an answer. The response must be correct 100% of the time to be correct.

When you have **qualifier words that allow for exceptions** such as **most, some, many, usually, seldom,** and **often**, there is a higher probability, the answer is correct because a response can be correct even when it is not correct 100% of the time.

Multiple Choice Question Strategy **Read both the question and answers With qualifier words in mind**	In the Julian Calendar, **every** year has **at least** how many calendar days? A **More Than** 366 days B **More Than** 367 days C **More than** 355 days D **More than** 365.5 days *(Bold print added for teaching purposes)*
Factor in the impact Of qualifier words	Qualifier Phases: **Every** = All, Having no exceptions **At least** = No less than **More Than** = Greater than

The qualifier words in the sample question make the selection
of the correct alternative an easy process.

Answer
A tricky question. **The answer is C,** every Julian calendar year, Leap Year, or Not, has over 355 days!

Based on Fact: The Julian Calendar 45BC has two types of years. Regular years of 365 days and every fourth year "leap years" of 366 days. The average Julian year is therefore 365.25 days.

Interesting Note: The Julian Calendar had an eight-day week. Our present calendar, The Gregorian or Christian calendar with its seven-day week, was first used in 1582.

TRUE/FALSE QUESTIONS

Method: Apply Strategies for True/False Questions

The fact that you have a 50/50 chance of being correct with True/False questions can give you a false sense of confidence. True/False questions can be difficult because it is not enough to know facts; you must also be able to interpret the statement as 100% true or not. A statement may appear true because most of it is true, but qualifier words and use of negatives can make the statement false.

TRUE: Requires the Answer be Always/Fully True, No Exceptions

FALSE: If Any Part Of The Statement Is False, The Entire Statement is False

---

True/False Question Strategy **Pay Attention To Details** **Look For Distortion In Details**	The Missouri Compromise was passed by Congress in 1822 **T/F**

The answer is **False**. 1822 is close but not 1820, the correct answer.

True/False Question Strategy **Focus On Qualifier Words To Determine If The Statement IS Always True or Not**	Given the constant barrage of commercials, often voters long for the election to be over. **T/F**

The answer is **True**. It is True because the word "often" allows for exceptions.

One method to help decide if the statement is True or False is to read the question without the identified qualifier word or words. You should then determine how the qualifier word influences what is True or False.

ESSAY QUESTIONS

Method: Understand What the Essay Answer Requires

Pause before you start to answer. Make sure you understand the question. What is being asked, what does the correct answer require? Are there multiple steps needed to answer the question?

Sample of Key Words
Action Words
Which Determine What Must be Part of the Answer

Analyze .... Identify underlying assumptions, discuss your opinion as to their accuracy.

Compare/and ...... What are the similarities and differences between two items.
Contrast

Critique .... An in-depth analysis and assessment of something, a critical evaluation.

Discuss .... Describe, talk about, elaborate, clarify aspects of the topic. Provide arguments for and against something.

Explain .... Provide factual knowledge and understanding of something. You can use a "What," "Why," and "How" approach to answering.

Evaluate/ .... Provide an assessment, critique that shares both positive and negative aspects.
Assess .... Express your opinion based on stated evidence.

EFFECTIVE STRATEGIES!

Learn And Apply
Test Taking Strategies

Method: Brainstorm Information For Answering Essay Question

Using keywords jot down the facts of what you know. Since this is brainstorming, you should not try to evaluate the value of the information on your list. This memory download process will serve the purposes of gathering information, and you will not have to expend mental energy, trying to remember each piece of information. You can add or delete to the list as you continue in the process of creating your essay response.

Sample Question and Brainstormed Information

Question: Discuss the explorer Christopher Columbus and his discovery of the "new world."

Brainstormed Information

Christopher Columbus   Italian

1492   Spain   National Holiday

A shorter route from Europe to Asia   seeking fame and fortune   Slavery

Landed in Caribbean   Queen Isabella   Not first to the Americas

Three ships - Nina, Pinta, Santa Maria

Method: Create An Outline From Your Brainstormed List

Creating an outline can be as simple as reflecting on your brainstormed list and numbering the order of presentation

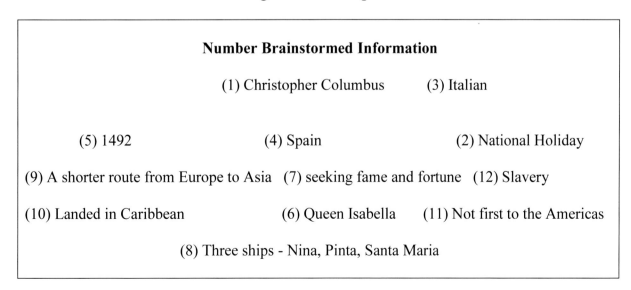

Number Brainstormed Information

(1) Christopher Columbus   (3) Italian

(5) 1492   (4) Spain   (2) National Holiday

(9) A shorter route from Europe to Asia   (7) seeking fame and fortune   (12) Slavery

(10) Landed in Caribbean   (6) Queen Isabella   (11) Not first to the Americas

(8) Three ships - Nina, Pinta, Santa Maria

Method: Write The Essay Focusing On Handwriting, Spelling, Grammar, and Sentence Structure

Regardless of the factual content in your essay, if it is neatly written, using proper mechanics of writing, it has a higher probability of being awarded a better grade.

Method: Read What You Have Written

If you read what you have written, you have the opportunity to correct simple mistakes like leaving out a word, misspellings, or verb-tense errors.

STANDARDIZED TESTS

Method: Become Familiar With Standardized Tests

Familiarity with the types of questions and structure of a standardized test will increase your score. Many students improve their scores on tests like the S.A.T.'s or G.R.E.'s, as much as ten percent (10%) when they take the test a second time because of the familiarity factor.

Preparation books and practice tests are available for most standardized tests at your local bookstore. If you use these resources to become familiar with the structure of a standardized test, you will know "what's coming," which can lower your anxiety and improve your performance. Taking practice tests can help you become familiar with the style of questions that you will need to answer. If, for example, you practice answering analogy questions, although you will not get the same analogies, you will be better able to think your way to the right answer.

Taking Practice Tests Can Improve Your Score

Method: Learn From Your Mistakes

When you analyze why you lost points on an exam, you can avoid the same mistake in future tests. If, for example, you missed multiple choice questions because you did not study textbook charts, you will be sure to do so for future exams. Perhaps you got an answer incorrect because you did not complete outside reading or had incomplete class notes. Your analysis might reveal that your preparation approach for essay questions was not adequate. If you are not sure why you lost points, talk to your teacher about the exam to gain an understanding of what you will need to do differently to get a better grade in the future.

Improve Your Test-Taking Skills
Learn From Your Mistakes

Discussion Questions:

How would you describe your test-taking skills?

How important do you consider the first test grade you receive in a course?

Recall a time that you lost points on an exam because you did not accurately follow the test directions?

What approaches do you use to make sure you have time to complete an exam?

What strategies do you use when completing Multiple Choice Questions?

What kind of questions do you prefer on a test -Multiple Choice, True/False, or Essay, why?

Describe your approach to answering essay questions?

NOTES

BONUS
LESSON

Methods to Help You

Develop
And
Maintain
Motivation

Lesson: Self-Motivation

Motivation = Process of Building Desire

Desire Leads to the Actions Needed For Better Grades

The Methods of Self-Motivation taught in this program will help you acquire the skills needed to develop and sustain the drive and commitment necessary to achieve good grades. There is "no magic" that will enable you to earn excellent grades without working for those grades. The enthusiasm and dedication you have to study will correspond to both your attitude toward learning and the rewards you identify from studying. This lesson will help you with periods of low motivation and help you overcome the challenge of procrastination.

"Study" in this program is a term that includes all activities that help you learn.

Motivation

Motivation is what provides you with a reason to do something; an incentive to take action.

Two sources of Motivation

Intrinsic Motivation refers to behaviors that you engage in for its own sake without the need for external rewards. The action itself is naturally enjoyable or satisfying to you.

Extrinsic Motivation refers to performance-driven behaviors that are stimulated by eternal rewards like grades, money, praise, awards, and employment opportunities.

Examples Of Motivation Sources in American History Course:

Intrinsic Motivation - You have a natural curiosity and interest in American history. You find it fun and exciting to learn about how the United States came to be, facts about the constitution, and facts about past presidents.

Extrinsic Motivation - You study to earn the highest grade possible, which will give you both pride and a sense of security. Obtaining a better grade will enable you to meet the requirements for your scholarships or athletic eligibility. Having a high-Grade Point Average (GPA) will lead to future educational opportunities and better employment opportunities.

It Will Be Easier To Commit Time And Energy Towards Study
If You Identify, Cultivate, And Focus On Both
Intrinsic And Extrinsic Sources Of Motivation.

Method: Focus On The Relationship Between Effective Study and Rewards

Benefits of Effective Study Habits

Better Grades: f you use the effective, efficient methods of academic study presented in this program, you will almost surely achieve better grades. If your grades are already excellent, there is a high probability that the skills taught in the program will make the process of earning A's or B's easier.

Less Anxiety: Using advanced study skills will give you confidence in your ability to learn and achieve good grades. State-of-the-Art study skills do not rely on last-minute cramming, which can be very uncomfortable and often do not work.

Gain More Knowledge: You want to learn and retain what you learn. Your approach to study should enable you to store new material in your long-term memory rather than in your short-term memory. When you retain what you have learned, you will have an advantage in future courses and when you take standardized tests such as the Scholastic Aptitude Test (S.A.T.), American College Test (A.C.T.), or post-college tests such as the Graduate Record Exam (G.R.E.).

Improve Self-image: A student who gets A's and B's has more pride. The positive self-image that comes from being a student who consistently earns good grades contributes to the confidence and comfort you have with peers, teachers, family members, and others. You think of yourself as smarter, and others judge you to be a more intelligent and capable person.

Increase Opportunities: The success you have in high school and college, measured primarily by grades, will enhance or limit your opportunities and choices. You will need good grades in high school, for example, to get into the most desirable colleges and universities or win scholarships. You will need good grades in college to have the best opportunities with employers or graduate schools. Colleges, graduate schools, and employers all prefer individuals who, along with other personal qualities, have demonstrated their ability to be successful. Good grades are the measure of academic success and your ability to succeed at what you attempt.

Method: Think Yourself to Success

"Who controls your thoughts?" The answer is that each of us controls our thoughts. How we choose to think is what generates our feelings. The will to study, the joy of learning, starts by having positive thoughts and feelings about the process and benefits of learning.

There will be some academic subjects that easily capture your interest, and that you view as fun to learn. There will be other academic subjects that require you to make an effort to develop a positive attitude for learning. If you are required to complete a course, it is counterproductive and self-defeating to take the approach that you have no control over your feelings. Maturity refers to your ability to understand and manage your emotions. Instead of giving in to negative thoughts toward the subject, strive to have a positive attitude toward the content that you need to learn. You will want to try to cultivate curiosity and interest in class topics; it will make the task of learning more enjoyable and manageable.

Method: Recognize that Commitment and Perseverance Are Required

There are many reasons not to succeed. You must recognize and overcome these challenges. The majority of the time, when students experience a "Lack of Academic Success," it is due to factors other than just ability. The most common reason for lack of success is not enough quality time spent on academic preparation. Finding enough time for academics is a challenge that all students face. The lessons in this program will teach you how to "Study Smart," making it possible for you to "Learn More" often in "Less Time."

**The Ability To Learn And Earn Good Grades Is Not Predetermined;
It Can Change With Effort.**

Method: Develop Short-Term and Long-Term Goals

Your educational goals should build on one another. The accomplishment of each goal is a step toward a bigger goal. You need to be specific when you define your short-term goals. For example, a short-term goal might be to make the honor roll in the present academic term by earning minimum grades of A in English, History, and Science and at least a B in each of your other subjects. Reaching this specific goal will require several sub-goals, such as a commitment to more study time and the use of better techniques.

Longer-term goals are also important but do not require the same degree of specificity. The goal of being eligible to attend a good university and obtain a college degree can be as powerful a motivator as the more defined goals of attending a particular university or getting a college degree leading to a specific career.

Goal Setting Tips

1. **Set goals that are realistic for you but make you reach beyond your current level of accomplishment.**

   If you are currently getting C's and B's in your academic subjects, resist becoming overly satisfied and comfortable with these grades. Use your imagination to visualize the increased satisfaction and opportunities you would have with better grades. If you firmly decide on the goal of A's and B's, you are more likely to accomplish this goal.

2. **Be specific with your short term goals.**

   When you have specific goals, you are less likely to rationalize and cut short the effort necessary to reach your goals.

3. **Write down your goals.**

   Written goals serve as a constant reminder. The formality of writing down your goals are akin to forming a contract with yourself for a specific action.

4. **Share your goals with others.**

   If, for example, you set the goal of making the honor roll this term, announce this to your parents or close friends you trust. When you share your goals, it puts positive pressure on you to produce what you have announced.

Method: Visualize the Accomplishment of Your Goals

An effective way to build desire is regularly to visualize the accomplishment of your goals. Take a few moments each day to relax and picture in your mind what it would be like to reach your goals. If, for example, your short-term goal is to make the honor roll this term, use your imagination to identify the joy and pride this accomplishment would bring you. Take the time to imagine yourself several years in the future and what your life would be like if you had consistently earned good grades. Visualize the positive feelings of success you will have when you graduate with good grades from high school, get accepted to the college of your choice, receive your college degree, and get selected for a dream job. It is also beneficial, although not pleasant, to visualize what the future would be like if you do not make use of effective study habits, and you receive poor grades. The negative feelings that come with visualizing not reaching your goals can be motivating when, in fact, you have the time to change the undesirable outcome with a better effort.

Other Life Goals

The study skills and habits suggested in this program do not require an excessive amount of time. The approaches to learning taught can enable you to study more efficiently and, therefore, give you more time for your other life goals. When you use proper planning methods, there can be plenty of time for fun. You will be more content and have a higher overall energy level if you have goals that call for an active personal and social life beyond academics.

Discussion Questions:

Why do you study?

What do you consider your most enjoyable subject? Why?

What do you view as the tangible benefits of studying short-term and long-term?

Describe a subject that you enjoy learning just for the sake of learning?

Can a person control their attitude toward the study of an academic subject? If so, how?

Describe ways you can develop a curiosity and interest in a subject?

Do you identify goals for achievement in courses when you start an academic term?

What approaches do you use to accomplish your goals?

NOTES

BIBLIOGRAPHY

Aguilar-Roca, N., Williams, A., O'Dowd, D. (2012). *The Impact of laptop-free zones on student performance and attitudes in large lectures.* Computers & Education, 59(4), 1300-1308.

Anderson, D., Gadaleto, A. (2007). *The College Alcohol Survey 1979-2006.* Retrieved from http://cehd.gmu.edu/assets/caph/CollegeAlcoholSurvey2007_pdf.pdf

Armstrong, W. (1975). Study Tips: How to Study Effectively and Get Better Grades. Woodbury, NY: Barron's Educational Series, Inc.

Armstrong, W., Lampe M. (1983). Study Tactics: A Master Plan for Success in School. Woodbury, NY: Barron's Educational Series. Inc.

Askov, E., Kamm, K. (1982). Study Skills in the Content Areas. Boston, MA: Allyn and Bacon

Bishop, J., Carter C., Kravitz, S. (2005) Keys To Success/Building Successful Intelligence for College, Career, and Life (5th ed.), Upper Saddle River, NJ: Pearson Education, Inc.

Boundless Psychology, (2016). *Memory Retrieval: Recognition and Recall.* Retrieved from https://courses.lumenlearning.com/boundless-psychology/chapter/step-3-memory-retrieval/

Bransford, J. (2000). How People Learn: Brain, Mind, Experience, and School. (Expanded Ed.). Washington, D.C.: National Academy Press.

Brown, W., Holtzman, W. (1972). A Guide to College Survival. Englewood Cliffs, NJ: Prentice Hall.

Carman, R., Adams, R. (1984). Study Skills: A Students Guide to Survival. New York, NY: John Wiley and Sons.

Centi, P. (1955). How to Study More Effectively. New York, NY: Fordham University Press.

Channing, L. (1988). About Making the Grade at College. South Deerfield, MA: Bete Co. Inc.

Chapman, E. (1974). College Survival. Palo Alto, CA: Science Research Associates

Cronbach, L. (1977). Educational Psychology (3rd Ed.). New York, NY: Harcourt Brace Jovanovich, Inc.

Dartmouth Academic Skills Center: *Learning Strategies*.(N.D.) Retrieved from https://students.dartmouth.edu/academic-skills/

Deese, J., Deese, E. (1979). How to Study (3rd Ed.). New York, NY: McGraw-Hill Co.

Dement, W. (1997). What All Undergraduates Should Know About How Their Sleeping Lives Affect Their Waking Lives. Standford University Center for Excellence for Diagnosis and Treatment of Sleep Disorders. Retrieved from http://web.stanford.edu/~dement/sleepless.html

Diet and Memory Tips to Boost Brain Power. Retrieved from http://www.memory-improvement-tips.com/diet-and-memory.html

Dobbin, J. (1984). How to Take a Test: Doing Your Best. Princeton, NJ: Educational Testing Service.

Educational Equality Project. (1983). Academic Preparation for College: What Students Need to Know and be Able to Do. New York, NY: College Board.

Fishel, J. (2015). Straight A's Are Not Enough. North Stuart, Fl: Flying Heron Books.

Franco, A. (2017). *Skipping Class* Retrieved from http://www.radford.edu/~archive/season05/life/stories/skipping.htm

Fried, C. (2008). *In-Class laptop use and its effects on student learning.* Computers and Education, 50, 906-914.

Friedman, M. (2014) *Notes on Note-Taking: Review of Research and Insights for Students and Instructors.* Harvard Initiative for Learning and Teaching. Retrieved from http://www.harvard.edu/searches?searchtext=NOTES%20ON%20NOTE-TAKING%3A#gsc.tab=0&gsc.q=NOTES%20ON%20NOTETAKING%3A&gsc.page=1

Furst, B. (1972). Stop Forgetting. Garden City, NY: Doubleday & Co.

Jobes, D. *(N.D.) Diet and Memory Tips to Boost Brain Power.* Retrieved from https://www.memory-improvement-tips.com/diet-and-memory.html

Glynn, S. et al. (2003). *Mnemonic Methods.* The Science Teacher pp 52-55. Retrieved from *http://search.proquest.com/docview/214619949)*

Go For It: High School Guidance Program Emphasis for "Excellence in Education. (1983). Guidance Department, Broward County: School Board of Broward County, Florida.

Good Diet, Exercise Keep Brain Healthy. (2008). Retrieved from https://www.livescience.com/2675-good-diet-exercise-brain-healthy.html

Graham, K., Robinson, H. (1985). Study Skills Handbook: A Guide for all Teachers. Newark, DE: International Reading Association.

Herold, M. (1982). *Memorizing Made Easy.* Chicago, IL: Contemporary Books, Inc.

Hitti, M. (2007). *Get Fit, Improve Memory.* Retrieved from http://www.webmd.com/fitness-exercise/news/20070313/get-fit-improve-memory#1

Hodson, P., Hodson, S. (1984) Studying Effectively and Efficiently. Toronto: University of Toronto.

How to Get the Most of Your College Education. (1981). New York: Association of American Publishers.

How to Get the Most Out of Your Textbook. (1981). New York: Association of American Publishers.

Jensen, E. (1979). You Can Succeed:The Ultimate Study Guide for Students. Woodbury, NY: Barron's Educational Series, Inc.

Jensen, E. (1982). Student Success Secrets. Woodbury, NY: Barron's Educational Series, Inc.

Kesselman-Turkel, J., Franklynn, P. (1981). Study Smarts: How To Learn More In Less Time. Chicago: Contemporary Books, Inc.

Kesselman-Turkel, J., Franklynn, P. (1981). Test Taking Strategies. Chicago: Contemporary Books, Inc., 1981.

Kesselman-Turkel, J., Franklynn, P. (1982). Note Taking Made Easy. Chicago: Contemporary Books, Inc.

Klosowski, T. (2013). *Back to Basics: Perfect Your Note-Taking Techniques.* Retrieved from https://lifehacker.com/back-to-basics-perfect-your-note-taking-techniques-484879924

Kornhauser, A. (1968). How to Study: Suggestions for High-School and College Students. Chicago Press.

Lakein, A. (1974). How to Get Control of Your Time and Your Life. New York, NY: Signet Book.

Mac Farlane, P., Hodson, S. (1984). Studying Effectively and Efficiently. Toronto, CA:
University of Toronto.

Maddox, H. (1963). How to Study. New York: Fawcett Premier Books.

National Youth Risk Behavior Survey (2009*). Alcohol and Other Drug Use and Academic
Achievement.* Retrieved from
https://www.cdc.gov/healthyyouth/health_and_academics/pdf/alcohol_other_drug.pdf

Nieves, L. (1984). Coping in College. Princeton, NJ: Educational Testing Service.

Pauk, W. (1984). How to Study in College. Boston, MA: Houghton Mifflin Co.

Paul, K. (2014). Study Smarter Not Harder. Bellingham, Washington: Self-Counsel Press.

Praveen, S. (2017). *Ebbinghaus Forgetting Curve,* Retrieved from
https://www.psychestudy.com/cognitive/memory/ebbinghaus-forgetting-curve

Preston, R., Morton, B. (1974). How to Study. Chicago, IL: Science Research Associates,
Inc.

Price, G., Griggs, S. (1985). *Counseling College Students through Their Individual
Learning Styles.* Ann Arbor, MI: Eric Counseling and Personnel Services Clearinghouse.

Psych Central. (2016) *Memory and Mnemonic Devices.* Retrived (January 2020) from
https://psychcentral.com/lib/memory-and-mnemonic-devices/

Raga, S.(2017). 7 Tips for How to Read Faster(and Still Understand What You Read). Retrieved
from https://www.mentalfloss.com/article/83881/how-to-read-faster

Sana, F., Weston, T., Cepeda, N. (2013.) *Laptop multitasking hinders classroom learning for
both users and nearby peers.* Computers & Education, 62, 24-31. Retrieved from
https://www.sciencedirect.com/science/article/pii/S0360131512002254

Sail on the Study Ship: Elementary Guidance Program Emphasis for "Excellence in Education"
(1983). Guidance Department, Broward County: School Board of Broward County,
Florida.

Shepherd, J. (1983). College Study Skills (2nd Ed.). Boston, MA: Houghton Mifflin Co.

Staton, T. (1982). How to Study, 7th ed. Unknown Binding

Study Skills Booklet for Adult Students. (N.D.). New York: Pace University Counseling and
Personal Development Center.

Tally, J., Henning, L. (1981). Study Skills: Establishing a Comprehensive Program at the College Level. Springfield, IL: Charles C. Thomas Publisher.

Tilus, G. (2012). *6 Critical Thinking Skills You Need to Master.* Retrieved from http://www.rasmussen.edu/student-life/blogs/main/critical-thinking-skills-you-need-to-master/

Wikipedia. *Explicit Memory.* Retrieved from
https://en.wikipedia.org/wiki/Explicit_memory

Wikipedia. *Memory Rehearsal* Retrieved from
https://en.wikipedia.org/wiki/Memory_rehearsal

Wikipedia. *Reading (process)* Retrieved from
https://en.wikipedia.org/wiki/Category:Reading_(process)

Wikipedia. *Short-Term Memory.* Retrieved from
https://en.wikipedia.org/wiki/Short-term_memory

Wikipedia. *Storage (Memory).* Retrieved from
https://en.wikipedia.org/wiki/Storage_(memory)

Wikipedia. *Subvocalization.* Retrieved from
https://en.wikipedia.org/wiki/Subvocalization

APPENDIX

FORMS

1. Time Schedule Worksheet

2. Master Task Schedule Worksheet

3. Daily Priority Schedule Worksheet

Forms May Be Copied

Time Management Worksheet   Proven Methods To Better Grades ®

Block (X)Time Reserved for Study   Weekly Study Time Goal_____Hours

	Monday	Tuesday	Wednesday	Thursday	Friday	Saturday	Sunday
8-9							
9-10							
10-11							
11-Noon							
Noon -1pm							
1-2pm							
2-3pm							
3-4pm							
4-5pm							
6-7pm							
7-9pm							
10-11pm							

Study Goal							
Actual Study							

Use Study Time for Homework, Preparation/Reading, Review, and Repetition.
Determine your weekly goal for "Time Reserved for Study."
Establish reserved times 6 or 7 days a week to reach your study time goals.
Develop a pattern of study, make studying at specific reserved times a habit.
If you miss a reserved block of study time, reschedule the lost time.

Method: Maintain a Master Task Schedule

A Master Task Schedule allows you to organize your academic tasks from a longer-term perspective and set realistic daily goals for study and review so you can complete all learning tasks and have adequate time for review before exams.

Master Task Schedule   Work Sheet

Subject	When Next Test Project Due	What Content To Be Tested	Reserved Review Days	Daily Task Goals
(Sample) History	*14 Days*	*Chapters 13 & 14 60 Pages*	*4 Days*	*Review Paper Project Plus Read Avg. 6 pages*

Method: Use A Daily Priority Schedule

When making use of a daily priority schedule, you review your goals from your Master Task Schedule and make adjustments based on your immediate needs. If, for example, you found out you were going to have a quiz the following day in science, you might postpone your daily goal in English and double your time spent in science. Often a review of your study needs for the day will lead to an increase in the time you commit to your academics.

Daily Priority Schedule   Work Sheet

Subject	Daily Goals From Master Task Schedule	Adjusted Goals Based on Priority Needs	Estimated Time To Complete	Notes
(Sample) **Science**	*Review Homework Plus Read*	*Quiz Tomorrow Review & Study Chapter 7*	*60 Minutes*	*Use time reserved for English*

Provenmethodstobettergades.com   Inquiries@provenmethods.net

Proven Methods To Better Grades

View Video Tutorials Online

provenmethodstobettergrades.com

**Available online
Video Program Introduction
Free Lesson Introduction Videos**

**If you wish to purchase the Video Program
Enter the $20 discount code below.**

PMB20

Proven Methods To Better Grades

View Video Tutorials Online

provenmethodstobettergrades.com

	Approximate Video Times	
	Introduction Video	**Methods Video**
Organization/Task Management	5 Minutes	19 Minutes
Memory Skills Part I	5 Minutes	20 Minutes
Concentration Methods	4 Minutes	9 Minutes
Time Management Skills	7 Minutes	13 Minutes
Reading For Speed & Retention	6 Minutes	21 Minutes
Classroom Skills	6 Minutes	12 Minutes
Note Taking Techniques	7 Minutes	16 Minutes
Memory Skills Part II	8 Minutes	16 Minutes
Papers And Projects	5 Minutes	16 Minutes
Controlling Test Anxiety	7 Minutes	12 Minutes
Test Taking Skills	7 Minutes	18 Minutes
Self-Motivation Techniques	8 Minutes	22 Minutes

Concentration Methods (Continued)

Time Management

Index Lesson Topics and Methods

Time Management (continued)

Method: Develop a Pattern of Study, P25

Method: Avoid Long Blocks of Study, P26

Method: (In College) Use Time Before, Between and After Class, P26

Method: Make Use of a Time Planner to Schedule and Monitor Your time, P 26

Reading For Speed and Retention

Readings is A Skill That Can Be Improved, P29

Method: Understand and Apply Strategies for Increasing Your Reading Speed, P29

How Focusing On More Words with Each Eye Fixation Can Increase Reading Speed, P30

Method: Practice Increasing Reading Speed, P30

Highlighting Textbooks, P30

Method: Apply Memory Steps with Academic Reading, P31

How to Read Academic Material, P31

Method: Vary Your Reading Speed, P 32

Classroom Skills

Method: Consider Class Attendance a Must-Do Activity, P35

Class Attendance is a Major Predictor of Academic Success, P 35

Method: Develop a Positive Attitude Toward Class, P 35

Method: Prepare for Class, P36

Classroom Skills (Continued)

Note-Taking

Papers, Projects, and Class Presentations (Continued)

Controlling Test Anxiety

Test-Taking Skills

Test-Taking Skills (Continued)

Self-Motivation